Items should be returned on or before the las [barcode: D1579713]
shown below. Items not already requested by
borrowers may be renewed in person, in writing or by
telephone. To renew, please quote the number on the
barcode label. To renew online a PIN is required.
This can be requested at your local library.
Renew online @ **www.dublincitypubliclibraries.ie**
Fines charged for overdue items will include postage
incurred in recovery. Damage to or loss of items will
be charged to the borrower.

**Leabharlanna Poiblí Chathair Bhaile Átha Cliath
Dublin City Public Libraries**

Comhairle Cathrach
Bhaile Átha Cliath
Dublin City Council

*Marino Branch
Brainse Marino
Tel: 8336297*

Date Due	Date Due	Date Due
JAN 18	06 FEB 20	
2 FEB 2019		

All marketing and publishing rights
guaranteed to and reserved by

FUTURE HORIZONS INC.

721 W. Abram St
Arlington, TX 76013
Toll-free: 800-489-0727
Phone: 817-277-0727
Fax: 817-277-2270
Website: www.FHautism.com
E-mail: info@FHautism.com

Printed in U.S.A.

Cover design: Maddie Coe
Interior design: David E. Brown

Children and teens depicted in photographs are models, not clients.. Photographs and graphics used under license. iPad photograph in chapter 6 by Michael Coté licensed under Creative Commons license 2.0. See https://creativecommons.org/licenses/by/2.0/legalcode. Photograph modified by the publisher..

ISBN 13: 978-1-941765-14-2

Contents

Introduction: Why This Book?   1

   Who should read this book?   2

   How to use this book   3

1   Some People Are More Anxious
   than Others   5

   Genetics and early temperamental differences   6

   Effects of a sensitive alarm system on thinking style   8

   Environmental stress   9

   Parenting style   10

2   Research Versus Practice:
   The Science and Art of Treatment   11

   The Science of Cognitive Behavioral Treatment (CBT)   11

   The science of neurobiological treatments   12

   Reducing environmental stressors   14

   The art of treatment in real practice   14

3   Getting Ready for Treatment: Motivating Change   17

   Step 1: Increase positive self-awareness   17

   Step 2: Learning about anxiety and FALSE ALARMS   19

   Step 3: Accept the presence of anxiety,
      but learn not to be controlled by it   20

4   Identifying Fears:
   Creating a Fear Ladder   21

   Step 1: Identify the type of feared situations   21

   Step 2: Create a "fear ladder"   27

Step 3: Give the client control of moving up the ladder 28

Step 4: Create a way to rate one's own level of anxiety 28

Step 5: Reward facing fears 29

5 Developing Tools to Lower Anxiety and Face Fears 31

Calming your worrisome thoughts (CBT strategies) 31

Calming your mind and body through exercise 34

Meditation, mindfulness-based stress reduction, relaxation 35

Putting it all together: Calming and facing fears. 57

6 Adapting Treatment for Less Verbal Children with Autism 61

Identifying their fears 62

Deciding whether to do exposure-based treatment or to simply change the
environment 63

Environmental supports for problems waiting, stopping something fun, or
dealing with a change 64

Modifying sensory challenges 65

Modifying difficult demands 66

Set up a fear ladder when it is not sensible to
avoid a situation 67

Explore tools to promote a relaxed state 70

7 Simple Phobia 73

8 Social Anxiety 77

9 Selective Mutism 85

10 Separation Anxiety and School Refusal 91

Jonathon 91

Mandy 97

11 Panic Disorder   101

12 Obsessive Compulsive Disorder   107

13 Somatic Symptom Disorder, and/or
   Illness Anxiety Disorder   115

14 Generalized Anxiety Disorder   121
   A Case of Perfectionism and College Admissions Anxiety   121

15 Other Common Fears   129
   Fear of others' aggression   129
   Fear of unexpected changes in schedule or routine   133

16 Summary of Key Points   137
   Treatment starts with motivation   137
   Identify specific fears and create a fear ladder   138
   Develop tools to help cope with and face fears   139
   Consider the big picture!   140
   The ultimate goal   141

References   143

Illustrations   146

Introduction: Why This Book?

There are many good books on helping children and young adults with anxiety. Numerous works spell out the key treatment components of programs proven to be effective in helping individuals face their fears and overcome debilitating anxiety. What they all have in common is the well-researched treatment protocol known as "gradual exposure." Study after study has shown that if you can get anxious individuals to gradually face their fears, their anxiety will decrease, and they will no longer be controlled by their fear. That is the science of treatment, to gradually face fears. That being said, how do you get someone with overwhelming anxiety to do just that? The art of treatment is figuring out what to do or say to persuade someone to gradually face his or her most dreaded fears.

Cognitive behavioral treatments offer some strategies to help children and teens face their fears. The primary method is to challenge anxious thoughts that serve to maintain fears and then provide rewards for gradually facing fears. For example, if a girl worries that a robber will come get her at night and refuses to be alone in her room, treatment would include reviewing the actual probability of such events to help her see that logically this is not likely to happen. The child would then be rewarded for gradually spending more and more time alone in her room. Treatment might also include strategies to help the body be calmer, including relaxation and physical exercises. All of these are tools to help an individual face fears.

The general idea of challenging anxious thoughts, using rewards and relaxation strategies to face fears is clear. What is not as clear is the exact words and strategies used to persuade a client to participate in treatment. In this book, I describe how to "win over" children and teens to partner with us in facing their debilitating fears. I try to give real life examples of the actual words and strategies used to motivate individuals to face a variety of common anxiety situations. Specifically, I describe what to do for simple phobias (e.g., fear of very specific things like dogs or bees); social anxiety; selective mutism; separation anxiety and school refusal panic disorder; obsessive compulsive disorder; somatic symptom disorder or illness anxiety disorder; generalized anxiety disorder; fear of others' aggression; anxiety due to unexpected changes; and fear of mistakes (perfectionism).

Who should read this book?

If you are a parent, teacher, or therapist with a child or teen whose anxiety interferes with the ability to function, then this book can help. Children with anxiety may not simply present with anxiety issues alone; they may have social or learning challenges that can lead to anxiety. They may have difficulty controlling impulses and their attention, which can lead to school and social difficulties that, in turn, lead to anxieties. A child may have an autism spectrum disorder that can contribute to difficulties with change, sensory challenges, and social and learning challenges. These can all contribute to heightened anxiety.

Many of the treatment strategies described in this book are appropriate for use with verbal children. You can use words to help them understand their anxiety and manage it. Exposure therapy (gradually facing one's fears) is the core component of anxiety treatment. For this, a facility with language is not needed. Chapter 6 shows how to adapt treatment to help children with more language challenges face their fears and lower their anxiety.

How to use this book

Those working with anxious children and teens, should learn about the general components of treatment described in chapters 1-5. For those working with children with severe autism, or children with less language comprehension, chapter 6 covers how to adapt treatment strategies with limited language.

After readers learn about the general components of treatment, they can look through chapters 7-15 to find case examples showing how treatment can be applied for specific types of fears.

In many ways, the strategies described in this book are not meant to be one-time strategies to "fix" an anxiety issue. These are tools one uses for life to help manage anxiety. This is not unlike the dieting world. Anyone can get on a diet to lose weight, but learning to eat better and exercise more are lifestyle changes that create lasting health. Those who struggle with anxiety issues, as described in chapter 1, may have a more sensitive system prone to anxiety reactions. Learning lifelong skills to manage these reactions is better than a quick, temporary fix.

The goal is to learn ways to manage anxiety so that the anxiety does not manage the individual. We all feel anxiety from time to time, yet we do not want it to lead to a pattern of avoidance and limit what we can do in our lives.

1 Some People Are More Anxious than Others

All of us have an alarm system to help us survive in the face of perceived danger. When a significant threat is detected, we are wired to react automatically with an intense emotional response to fight, flee, or freeze as if our lives depended on it. Daniel Goleman, in his book *Emotional Intelligence*, refers to these moments as a state of being "hijacked by emotions" (Goleman, 1995). It is as if the emotion center has taken over the rest of the brain so that we don't have easy access to our reasoning ability.

Some people refer to this as the "crocodile" or "reptilian" brain taking over. The human brain has both the remnants of the old reptilian brain (particularly the limbic system), which controls this "fight-or-flight response," and the newer, human part of the brain, called the neocortex, which is associated with planning and reasoning ability. When threatened, our reptilian brain may cause us to flee, fight, or freeze without the cerebral cortex intervening (i.e., without our ability to reason or think about what we are doing). This quick, non-thinking response certainly has survival value. In a truly dangerous situation, we may not have time to contemplate our actions. We swiftly move away from the danger, hide out, or fight back.

For example, when walking down the street, if a car suddenly veers off the road onto the sidewalk into your direction, this is not a time to reflect. You must move quickly to a safer place. This is a TRUE ALARM. Yet in a world where perceived threats may not always be life threatening, the fight, flight, or freeze response can lead to FALSE ALARMS, causing us to become emotionally reactive when no actual danger is present.

Why would some people have a more sensitive alarm system that may lead to more false alarms?

Genetics and early temperamental differences

Although anyone can feel threatened and become emotionally reactive, some of us may be born with a more sensitive alarm system than others. Genetic studies show that anxiety disorders do run in families, and if an individual has an anxiety issue, there is a greater likelihood that some family members also have had anxiety issues.

Long-term studies (from infancy through childhood) show that most individuals are born with a recognizable and persistent temperament. Some folks are easy going, others quite slow to warm up, and others more likely to show greater negative emotional reactions to new situations. Thomas and Chess (1977), in their now-famous studies of newborns, examined nine key dimensions of behavior:

1. Activity level

2. Rhythmicity (e.g., schedule of feeding, sleep, and elimination)

3. Approach/withdrawal patterns

4. Adaptability

5. Threshold of responsiveness

6. Intensity of reaction

7. Quality of mood

8. Distractibility

9. Attention span and persistence

Based on these nine dimensions, Thomas and Chess were able to characterize about 60% of children into one of three categories and show that these patterns of behavior were often quite stable over time. The first category is the "easy child" who can accept frustration with less fussiness, maintain a more positive mood, and easily adapt to change.

The second is the difficult child. He shows a more negative response to new situations and has more intense crying and tantrums when frustrated. The last is the "slow-to-warm-up child." He initially shows a mild negative reaction to new situations, but gradually adapts with more exposure to those situations. Both the "difficult child" and "slow-to-warm-up child" are more likely to be prone to anxiety and emotional reactivity. Although these patterns seem to be stable characteristics, parental response can alter a child's temperament. For example, work by Kagan (1994) shows that timid youngsters who are gently encouraged to be more outgoing by their parents—and thus are gradually exposed to new situations—become less fearful.

Although having a difficult or slow-to-warm-up temperament does not mean one has a "behavior disorder," certain disorders are associated with greater levels of emotional reactivity. Children with anxiety disorders, attention deficit hyperactivity disorder (ADHD), and some mood disorders (such as bipolar disorder) may have greater difficulty controlling their emotional reactions. In addition, those with autism spectrum disorders and sensory processing disorders may have greater challenges in handling new situations and prefer repetitive routines.

Effects of a sensitive alarm system on thinking style

Those who are more emotionally reactive to potential dangers will often develop hypervigilance to such threatening situations. In other words, they may tend to focus much more on the potential for harm and anger. Their thoughts tend to be dominated by anxious worry because they frequently anticipate their own reactivity. Studies show that anxious individuals are much more likely to develop an anxiety-prone cognitive style that overinflates the probability and severity of anticipated negative events (Uhlenhuth et al, 2002; Rapee et al, 2008).

The good news is that treatment can potentially reverse these negative thinking styles. Exposure therapy can help individuals realize that dreaded expected events do not happen with the probability or severity anticipated.

Environmental stress

In addition to inborn temperament and thinking style, certain environmental factors can contribute to heightened sensitivity to threats and fear. Traumatic stressful events can lead to a variety of negative outcomes, including heightened anxiety, depression, and subsequent drug use.

Not all stressful events lead to trauma. Research suggests that prolonged inescapable stress leads to worse outcomes. For example, getting robbed once could certainly be traumatic, yet living in a war zone or in certain crime-ridden environments exposed to constant stressors with no way to escape is likely to have a more traumatizing effect. Chronic family conflicts, abuse, or neglect are examples of prolonged stressors that can raise the risk of anxiety disorders.

Parenting style

Protecting children from REAL DANGERS is crucial. However, when families enable their children to avoid non-dangerous, yet feared, situations, they create a higher risk of developing problematic anxiety. For example, allowing kids to avoid going to a supportive school or interacting with kind peers can lead to worsening anxiety.

If parents have their own high levels of anxiety, this can influence how much they allow their child to face his or her fears. It may be more difficult for parents with high levels of anxiety to tolerate seeing their child feeling the same way. The tendency may be to protect the child from this discomfort. With education, parents can learn when a situation is a true danger, and when it would be better to encourage their children to face a feared situation.

2 Research Versus Practice: The Science and Art of Treatment

Researchers and therapists often have different goals, yet both inform each other. Researchers often seek to evaluate a treatment approach; therapists seek to help a particular client. When doing research, certain clients may be ruled out if they do not fit the criteria for the study. As a clinician or a parent, the client or kid you see is the one you treat. As researchers design and evaluate treatment protocols, therapists and parents have to modify those protocols to fit the needs of their clients or kids. Thus, there is the science generated from the research, and the art of practice where such treatments are used in real life settings.

The Science of Cognitive Behavioral Treatment (CBT)

Much research (see Barlow, 2004) has demonstrated that a key component of effective anxiety reduction is gradual exposure to the feared situation until an individual learns that nothing bad happens. When a person has a false alarm, the only way to learn that it is a false alarm is to confront the situation long enough to discover it is safe. Therefore part of the science of anxiety reduction is a behavioral treatment called "gradual exposure therapy."

Cognitive behavioral treatments help individuals to approach feared situations by trying to alter their anxious thoughts. Individuals are asked to assess the actual evidence for their anxious thoughts. This helps to curb the tendency to overestimate the probability and consequences of negative or harmful events. We ask clients to behave like scientists, using their rational minds to collect data on the real probability of danger rather than letting their emotions rule their behavior. Young clients are also rewarded for facing each step of a feared situation.

The science of neurobiological treatments

A variety of physical activities and treatments can also reduce anxiety and stress. Several medications can directly reduce feelings of anxiety and depression. These typically include both the class of medications called anti-depressants and anxiolytic medications that directly reduce anxiety. The problem with some anxiolytics is that they immediately reduce anxiety and produce a feeling of calm that can become addictive for many. Anxiolytics, like the benzodiazepines, can lead to classic addiction symptoms, including tolerance and withdrawal effects. Individuals may need larger doses over time to get the same effects, thus creating larger negative side effects over time. Because of these difficulties, many of the antidepressants (like the SSRIs) may be used instead of anxiolytics as they can reduce anxiety without classic signs of addiction. However, as with all medications, the SSRIs may have negative side effects, including weight gain and problems with sexual performance for some patients.

A variety of alternatives to medication exist that can directly reduce anxiety. Numerous studies have shown aerobic exercise to be as effective as some of the antidepressant medications in reducing anxiety and depression while increasing confidence and energy (Blumental et al, 1999). Meditation, including mindfulness meditation, has also been shown to have positive effects on stress and anxiety reduction—even in school children (Meiklejohn, et al., 2012). Many of these activities share a common theme of focusing on something in the moment (breathing, a body sensation) rather than attending to anxious thoughts about the past or future. These strategies can produce a feeling of well-being and relief from chronic worrying.

Another non-pharmacological treatment to reduce anxiety that has received some positive results is neurofeedback (e.g., Hammond, 2005). Neurofeedback (NFB) is a form of biofeedback, in which brainwaves (EEG patterns) are assessed and connected to a video game. The video game provides rewarding feedback when targeted brain wave patterns are achieved. In this way, neurofeedback can train the brain to produce certain types of brain wave patterns associated with relaxation, increased focus, or other targeted states.

Reducing environmental stressors

A crucial part of treating anxiety is identifying larger stressors that may be influencing specific symptoms. For example, Chris was a child who compulsively washed his hands to relieve fears about germs. He met the criteria for obsessive compulsive disorder. Standard treatment involved gradual exposure therapy where he would get his hands dirty and then be prevented from washing them for a period of time to learn that nothing bad would happen. However, in taking a step back to look at the history of his symptoms, we discovered that his hand washing increased when entering a new school that made much greater work demands. When his work load was reduced in line with what he could handle, the symptoms of hand washing decreased. The point here is to pay attention not only to specific symptoms, but also to the client's larger life context in order to determine which stressors may be contributing to fluctuations in anxiety symptoms.

The art of treatment in real practice

Armed with knowledge about how to treat anxiety, how do we now get a child and, or his family motivated to try these treatment strategies? Remember, we are asking kids to do the most difficult thing: face their fears!

Good therapists spend time winning over their clients rather than dictating a protocol to treat anxiety. Developing trust, hope, and then partnering with the child to motivate him to reduce the anxiety is crucial. Remember, not all individuals who are dragged into treatment by their families want to address their anxiety symptoms. The next chapter describes the steps that I take in trying to "win over" my clients to join me in helping them to reduce the negative effects of their anxiety.

3 Getting Ready for Treatment: Motivating Change

Step 1: Increase positive self-awareness

Therapy can be threatening, especially if you are being forced into it by others. There is an unspoken message that something is wrong with you that needs to be fixed. I prefer to begin therapy with what is right about my clients to help them see their value and feel optimistic about their future. From this position of strength we can talk about challenges that get in the way (like anxiety symptoms).

I start by explaining that everyone has a profile of strengths and challenges. Therefore, to get to know them, it would be helpful to map out their profile. Be-

gin by making a list of their strengths (at least 7) and a smaller list of challenges (3 and under). Strengths include any special knowledge, traits, and characteristics they possess. One strength that many individuals with anxiety typically have is a great capacity to understand the pain of others. This is an important talent that allows them to be great friends, partners, or coworkers. (See sample profile for Joe on following page.)

Strengths are things that lead to successful careers and relationships. Joe's strengths (shown below) can lead to a successful school experience and perhaps a

Joe's Profile

Strengths	Challenges (caused by Sensitive alarm system)
Great memory	Fear of making mistakes
Vast knowledge of history	Speaking in front of class
Great factual knowledge about animals	Meeting new people
Good at math and science	
Empathic – caring and understanding of others	
Good piano player	
Good video game player	
Excellent swimmer	
Total 8	**Total 3**

career in education, science, or working with animals. His caring attitude and other interests will also allow him to be a very good friend to others.

Challenges are things that can get in the way of reaching those goals. For Joe, his anxieties could get in the way of his great academic pursuits or even making friends if he is not careful. We do not need to totally overcome challenges; we just need to get "good enough" so they are no longer in our way. It is easier to digest the need to change anxiety symptoms when they are no longer a threat to our entire being. They are just a smaller, compartmentalized part of ourselves that we need to alter a bit so it does not interfere with the rest of us.

Step 2: Learning about anxiety and FALSE ALARMS

Teach the client about the alarm system we all have to keep us safe. Our limbic system is the alarm that responds to danger by readying us for fight or flight (or freeze). Adrenaline pumps, and we are ready to run, hide, or, if there is no escape, to fight. This causes our heart to pound, our brow to sweat, our breathing to become rapid, and our muscles to tense (among other reactions). I also explain that we can have TRUE or FALSE alarms. A TRUE ALARM is when there is in fact a real danger, such as a car about to hit us. A FALSE ALARM is when there is no real danger (as in calling a kind friend on the telephone), but we think there is, and react as if our lives were in danger. Some of us inherit a more sensitive alarm system that can set off many FALSE ALARMS. In our sessions, we often discuss other family members who may have also had a sensitive alarm system. The point is to help clients understand that although their alarm reactions are real bodily responses and are not made up, the danger is typically not real and represents a FALSE ALARM.

Step 3: Accept the presence of anxiety, but learn not to be controlled by it

Rather than trying to get rid of anxious thoughts, we can explain that those thoughts are like a TV going on in the background much of the time. Controlling one's mind entirely is difficult. So, the noise of those anxious thoughts will be there, but because most are FALSE ALARMS, we have to learn not to be controlled by those thoughts. We can examine whether there really is or is not a danger, and resist the urge to avoid the anxious situation. We can learn to face our fears even if we cannot get rid of the scary feeling.

Years ago, I made my first public speech. I was filled with anxiety, worried the audience would think I did not know my subject, or, worse yet, that I was a big bore. I realized the worry might be a false alarm, but my lack of confidence had me hold on to the possibility that I was in real danger of humiliation. I was just starting my career and realized I needed to make a living even if I was no good at it. Maybe the fear of not working was worse than the fear of being humiliated. So I did the talk. It went okay – not great – not humiliating either. It was enough of an exposure without the anticipated horrible consequences to have me do it again. I eventually made public speaking a regular and successful part of my career.

4 Identifying Fears: Creating a Fear Ladder

Step 1: Identify the type of feared situations

This is crucial since treatment will focus on gradual exposure to the very things that are feared. Sometimes, what is feared is not just the original fear, but a secondary fear. For example, in obsessive compulsive disorders, a child may fear getting sick with a germ from a dirty door knob, which would lead him to wash his hands. The initial fear may be dirt, but the secondary fear becomes anything that would interfere with his access to washing his hands. Thus, treatment needs to focus not only on touching door knobs, but also tolerating greater amounts of time without washing hands.

The *Diagnostic and Statistical Manual of Mental Disorders*, 5th Edition (DSM-5™, American Psychiatric Association, 2013) describes the symptoms of various anxiety disorders, which are generally categorized around a particular target of the fear, or the ways in which people avoid those fearful situations.

For simple phobias, the targeted fear is straightforward; the person can identify a specific thing (e.g., dogs, bees, or swimming) that triggers anxiety. For other disorders, identifying the exact fear is trickier.

In social phobia, individuals are afraid of interacting in public for fear of being embarrassed or humiliated by their own actions. They may avoid speaking in public, using public restrooms, eating with other people, or engaging in social contact in general. Many children or teens with social phobia are quite isolated, fearful of reaching out to connect with peers.

In selective mutism, the fear is about talking to others despite having the ability to talk. Children may refuse to talk with their teacher or peers and yet talk quite openly to their parents or siblings at home.

For those with separation anxiety, fear of being alone or away from a trusted parent/guardian is often the key issue. The DSM-5 describes it as follows:

Separation anxiety disorder consists of persistent and excessive anxiety beyond that expected for the child's developmental level (lasting at least four weeks for children) related to separation or impending separation from the attachment figure (e.g., primary caregiver, close family member) as evidenced by at least three of the following criteria:

- Recurrent excessive distress when anticipating or experiencing separation from home or from major attachment figures

- Persistent and excessive worry about losing major attachment figures or about possible harm to them, such as illness, injury, disasters, or death

- Persistent and excessive worry about experiencing an untoward event (e.g., getting lost, being kidnapped, having an accident, becoming ill) that causes separation from a major attachment figure

- Persistent reluctance or refusal to go out, away from home, to school, to work, or elsewhere because of fear of separation

- Persistent and excessive fear of or reluctance about being alone or without major attachment figures at home or in other settings

- Persistent reluctance or refusal to sleep away from home or to go to sleep without being near a major attachment figure

- Repeated nightmares about separation

- Repeated complaints of physical symptoms (e.g., headaches, stomachaches, nausea, vomiting) when separation from major attachment figures occurs or is anticipated

— DSM-5, 2013

There are children who have a phobia of school without separation anxiety. In these cases, the child can separate from a parent, yet avoids school because of stressors related to the school environment, such as teasing or overwhelming academic demands.

In panic disorder, the fear is related to having a panic attack. A panic attack is a surge of intense fear or discomfort that resembles an exaggerated alarm response. It is characterized by at least four of the following symptoms: heart pounding palpitations; sweating; trembling; shortness of breath or smothering feelings; feelings of choking; chest pain or discomfort; nausea or abdominal distress; feeling dizzy or lightheaded; chills or heat sensations; numbing or tingling sensations; feelings of being detached from oneself or reality; or fear of losing control, going crazy, or dying. A panic attack itself is not a disorder, but if it is followed by at least one month of fear of having another one, or avoiding situations because a person fears he or she will have another attack, then that becomes an anxiety disorder. Some develop agoraphobia after panic attacks. This refers to a fear of going outside the home due to the concern of having a panic attack in a public place where they will not be able to hide or get help. Thus, the key fear in panic disorder, with or without agoraphobia, is the fear of having a panic attack, or the fear of one's own alarm response.

In generalized anxiety disorder, the individual has persistent worries (for at least six months) about a number of events or activities, such as school or work performance. Though the fears are more diffuse than in a simple phobia, the approach to treatment is similar. One needs to learn from the child what the specific areas of worry are. Listening carefully to the types of worries the child discusses will help dictate what thoughts to challenge and what fearful situations to help the child face.

Other related disorders are somatic symptom disorder and illness anxiety disorder. In these disorders, there may be a real physical symptom, but the worry about it and the time and energy devoted to caring for this symptom (or preventing illness) is excessive.

In obsessive compulsive disorder, individuals have either obsessions, compulsions, or both. Obsessions are recurrent, intrusive, and unwanted thoughts, urges, or images causing the individual to feel distress. The individual may try to ignore them or neutralize them with a compulsive action.

Compulsions are maladaptive repetitive actions that aim to reduce the anxiety or distress brought on by an obsession. Typical examples: compulsively washing hands to undue the anxiety associated with obsessive fears of germs; checking doors, locks, or appliances to undo the fear that something was left open or on that could result in danger.

Another type of obsession is called morbid obsessive thoughts. This is when individuals may have thoughts or urges of hurting or harming others or committing what they believe to be inappropriate behaviors. Instead of acting on such thoughts, they are quite distressed by them. Such morbid thoughts may be accompanied by compulsive behaviors, such as praying, counting, or other superstitious behaviors thought to control the obsession. Or, affected individuals may avoid people or situations in which they fear they may act inappropriately. These are not individuals who are planning to hurt or harm others, but rather have disturbing thoughts and are quite distressed by them.

There are several other anxiety-related fears that do not fit neatly into any anxiety disorder description in the DSM-5 system. Instead, these may be part of, or associated with, a variety of anxiety disorders. One of these is the fear of other people's aggression. I have worked with several sensitive individuals who have a stronger than usual fear response to witnessing others getting briefly or mildly angry or acting in unexpected ways. They are often afraid the other person will hurt them directly, hurt others, or act so poorly that they will be punished by others. All elicit anxiety that may cause individuals to avoid situations in which those people may be found. Treatment often involves challenging the thoughts that another person's brief and mild anger will result in any harm.

Another common anxiety, especially for those on the autism spectrum, is fear of changes in routine. For those with limited problem-solving skills, any new situation can create anxiety because the individuals are not confident in their ability to cope with the new circumstances. Treatment often involves learning that even when things change, most things remain the same. For any unexpected change, there are always people willing to help.

Lastly, perfectionistic thinking underlies many anxiety-related problems, like fear of making a mistake, being corrected, or losing a game. Somehow, these situations are seen as a reflection of the individual's competence or intelligence and lead to humiliation and subsequent avoidance of situations in which he may perform less than perfectly.

Such behavior makes it difficult for these individuals to learn anything new because the risk of mistakes is higher. Treatment focuses on challenging the belief that mistakes reflect insufficient abilities or intelligence. Instead, treatment promotes the idea that mistakes are an essential part of learning something new.

Step 2: Create a "fear ladder"

For each type of fear, make a list of situations from least fearful to most fearful. Then the child can gradually face those fears. Rapee et al. (2008) call these lists "fear ladders." Each rung of the ladder represents another step towards overcoming fear and anxiety. For example, my clients who are afraid of arranging a get-together with a peer might break up the task into smaller steps ("rungs on the ladder"); for example, just say "Hi" at lunch. At another time, find out which video games they both like, then another time ask for a phone number in case they want to talk about video games, and then ask the peer if he or she wants to hang out to play video games. Finally, have the get-together.

Step 3: Give the client control of moving up the ladder

Facing fears is scary business, and no one should feel forced into it. There is a difference between coercion and encouragement. As my client and I both examine whether a fear response is really a FALSE ALARM, it is up to the client to decide when he or she is ready to face the feared situation. I will do all in my power to help a client see the evidence that a feared situation is much less dreadful than imagined, yet it is up to the child to decide when he or she is ready to face that situation. Each rung of the ladder, the client decides what step to try.

Step 4: Create a way to rate one's own level of anxiety

It is crucial for individuals to see for themselves how their anxiety level actually decreases after sufficient exposure to feared situations. This helps reinforce that they were having a FALSE ALARM, and that over time, they will become calmer in the face of those situations as they learn nothing bad happens.

The name of such rating systems have ranged from Subjective Units of Discomfort (for adults) to the Stress Meter (for kids). In either case, one can use a 5 point scale such as the one below, to rate one's anxiety before and after facing a fear.

Step 5: Reward facing fears

There are two broad categories of rewards for facing fears: intrinsic rewards and extrinsic rewards. Intrinsic rewards are the naturally occurring rewards for facing fears. Feeling pride and knowing that you are able to do so much more than you used to do, are intrinsic rewards of facing fears. We can help clients see the payoff of being able to break out of their patterns of avoidance. We can help them feel proud of themselves for no longer letting anxiety control them.

Extrinsic rewards refer to providing an artificially created reward after facing a fear. This might be something like getting to play a video game or purchasing special items as a reward for taking a step towards facing a fear. For younger kids, and those students with greater cognitive challenges who may not comprehend the intrinsic payoff of overcoming anxiety, external rewards may be especially useful to motivate change.

5 Developing Tools to Lower Anxiety and Face Fears

There are many tools that can be used specifically in preparation for, during, and after exposure sessions. Cognitive Behavioral Treatment (CBT) focuses on changing specific worrisome thoughts. Meditation and mindfulness strengthen one's ability to attend to the here and now rather than experience the constant swirl of worry about the past or the future. Exercise and physical activity may help to distract from constant worry and create greater blood flow to reasoning parts of the brain, increase the production of chemicals that improve mood, and decrease inflammatory processes that worsen mood.

Calming your worrisome thoughts (CBT strategies)

The basic concept of CBT for anxiety is to use logic and scientific reasoning to challenge the validity of the worrisome thoughts that maintain a high state of anxiety. There are a variety of strategies described in the CBT literature, including identifying automatic anxious thoughts, analyzing the kinds of mistakes (or cognitive distortions) represented in those anxious thoughts, and developing alternative, more reasonable thoughts. We often ask clients to keep a record of both their anxious thoughts and alternative thoughts that are generated in therapy sessions. In practice, I have found that kids may feel burdened by some of this recording. Trying to identify the exact distortions represented in their anxious thoughts can become more of an academic exercise than a therapeutic one.

To simplify matters for children, Rapee et al. (2008) distills the large number of cognitive distortions to just two that are most often represented in a child's anxious thinking: overestimating the probability of negative events or overestimating the consequences of those negative events, or both. We can highlight these two issues to help kids generate more reasonable, less worrisome thoughts.

The essence of CBT is to behave like a scientist and collect evidence to determine the actual probability and/ or consequences of anticipated negative events. For example, as a frequent flier, I have had my share of fears of being in a plane crash after watching reports of horrible crashes. Yet as a scientist, I can look up statistics on the total number of flights and the number of crashes in a year to discover how ridiculously low the probability of crashing on a commercial flight really is. The probability is just 1 in 4.7 million that any one of us would die in a plane crash on one of the 78 major airlines. The odds are closer to 1 in 20 million if you only fly the top 39 airlines, which have even better safety records.[1]

---

1   Source: OAG Aviation & PlaneCrashInfo.com accident database, 20 years of data (1993 - 2012)

When it comes to challenging kids' worries about the consequences of anticipated negative events, we can help them by asking, "What is the worst that can happen?" Then examine whether the worst would even be so bad. For example, a child may be afraid to make a speech in front of his class for fear of making a mistake. We could then ask, "So what if you did make a mistake? What would happen? What usually happens if someone makes a mistake in class?" We could continue in this line of thinking until the child realizes that a mistake would not spell the end of his school career nor even a bad grade on the project. It might even make him more relatable to other kids who will also make mistakes.

I prefer to excuse kids from copious record keeping of their anxious and alternative thoughts. Instead, write a summary for them of ways to "Think Like a Scientist." (See the summary below regarding the two examples I previously discussed regarding fear of flying and fear of talking in the classroom). This kind of summary can remind kids of more realistic thinking before facing a fear.

Think Like a Scientist

Feared situation	Anxious thought	Realistic outcome
Flying	I might die in a crash	Chances are 1 in 4 million or 1 in 20 million on the best 39 airlines. So it's not going to happen.
Doing a speech in class	Might mess up	Mistakes are expected, they will not drastically bring down a grade, and many kids appreciate some mistakes as it takes the pressure off them.

Calming your mind and body through exercise

Exercise and other physical activities are excellent strategies to reduce anxiety and depression. Madhukar H. Trivedi, a professor of psychiatry at the University of Texas Southwestern Medical Center in Dallas, has demonstrated in many studies the positive effects of exercise on mood, both in the short term (hours after exercise) and in maintaining positive moods for longer periods for those who exercise regularly. Several studies show exercise to be at least as effective as antidepressant medications (Blumental et al, 1999). It seems that aerobic exercise may have the largest effect, followed by weight training. Other studies have shown yoga improves mood. Therefore, many experts recommend that individuals with anxiety begin a regular exercise program, particularly one that involves an aerobic component, such as jogging, walking, swimming, biking, or other sports that require aerobic activity.

There are times, however, when it is not possible to be physically active, such as when confined during travel or when going to bed at night. Therefore, we need ways to calm ourselves when our bodies are quieter. Meditation and mindfulness stress reduction embrace strategies to bring calmness to mind and body in a way that does not depend on movement.

Meditation, mindfulness-based stress reduction, relaxation

These practices involve learning to focus one's attention to what's happening in the moment, whether something experienced with the five senses (such as a taste, smell, sound, touch, or sight) or an internal sensation, such as the feeling of one's breathing or even the awareness of having a particular thought or anxiety sensation. By focusing on the moment at hand, one no longer focuses on a feared future event or regrets of a past event. Periods of time allocated to focusing the mind on the present moment are associated with a sense of well-being and reduced anxiety. This is as if the action of the forebrain (and its ability to observe experience) short circuits the ability of the limbic system to hijack the rest of the brain.

Though "mindfulness" is considered more a way of trying to live one's life rather than a specific tool, there are some activities that can help sharpen the mind's ability to have greater awareness of the moment, thereby reducing anxiety.

I have included four scripts that parents or teachers can use to guide their children through these meditative practices. Although the first technique was not initially considered a mindfulness meditation, it certainly fits our current understanding of mindfulness in its focus on immediate sensory experience. The technique was first described by Dr. Edmund Jacobson in his 1929 book, *Progressive Relaxation.* Progressive relaxation, also known as Jacobsonian Relaxation, involves the tensing, and then relaxing, of the muscles of the body, one group at a time. As individuals notice the contrast between tensing and relaxing muscles, they are better able to create a state of relaxation.

The second script describes a technique for deep breathing. Anxiety is often associated with short, rapid breaths. Deep breathing, on the other hand, is associated with a relaxed state. Learning to breathe deeply can help induce a state of relaxation, and because it helps the individual to focus on an immediate sensory experience, it can shift attention away from the constant swirl of worrisome thoughts.

The third script is a mindfulness exercise to help youngsters become more aware of their immediate sensory experience. It uses a raisin or another similar food item in order to help focus attention to smell, taste, sound, sight, and touch.

The last script is a guided mindfulness meditation, turning inward to focus on one's breathing (without trying to alter it), and awareness of wandering thoughts with a refocus on breathing.

Parents, counselors, or teachers can use these scripts with kids to help find regular ways of relaxing. In addition, there are a growing number of free guided audio mediations available online and through apps for smart phones and tablets. By the time you read this book, there will be many more, but here are some I have found useful:

Online: www.fragrantheart.com, look for the meditations for children.

Apps

- Take a Chill

- Sleep Meditations for Kids

- Smiling Mind

- Calm

- The Mindfulness App

- Simply Being

- Buddhify

The interested reader will find many more by searching for "free meditation guides" online.

Script 1
A Progressive Muscle Relaxation for Children

Let's get quiet and comfortable. You can sit in a chair or lie on your back. Let your body get loose like a spaghetti noodle. Close your eyes, if you can, to help you relax. We are going to work on relaxing different parts of your body.

Let's start with your hands and arms

Pretend there is a rope attached to a giant rock. You need to grab the rope in each hand to move the rock. You need to grab on tight and make a fist so the rope won't slip out of your hands. Now pull hard with your hands to try to move the rock. Feel your arms and hands get tight. Now just let go of the rope and let your hands and arms fall like a noodle again. Notice how nice and relaxed your hands and arms feel. Let them just flop loosely by your side.

Now let's do your face

Try to make a really angry face. Scrunch up your nose. Show your teeth and squeeze your eyes shut. Hold that angry look and feel how tight your face feels. Now let it go, let your face fall and smooth out. Feel your whole body relax now as you let go and just relax.

Now let's move to your tummy

Imagine that a silly friend of yours is going to sit on your tummy. You need to tighten your tummy so the weight won't crush you. Make your tummy hard to hold your friend's weight for a moment. Now your friend gets off and you can let your tummy relax and get soft like jelly. You can breathe easily and feel your body relax .

Now let's focus on your legs and feet

Pretend that you are trying to stretch your legs and feet to make them longer. Point your toes and straighten your legs and stretch them as far as they will go. Try to hold that position for a moment. Now just let your feet and legs relax. Let them go limp like a noodle. Feel the difference between the stretch and how relaxed your legs are now.

Now let your whole body become a noodle and let all your muscles relax. Take a deep breath in and let all the tension out. Remember this nice feeling whenever you want to relax again. When you are ready, you can open your eyes and slowly let your body move again.

Script 2 Deep Breathing to Relax

We are going to take some big deep breaths in order to help us feel less stress. When we take deep breaths, our bellies get bigger when the air comes in, and then our bellies flatten out when we breathe out. Let's get ready to try this.

Let's get comfortable by lying on our backs. If you are not in a place where you can lie on your back, you can just sit comfortably. Make sure your belly has plenty of room to get big and small. Rest a hand gently on your belly so you can feel when it gets big and small.

Now, take a big breath in through your nose (you can use your mouth too if you are stuffy). Breathe in slowly and count to five in your head. Feel your belly rise as the air comes in. The air is good for your body.

Then, slowly breathe out, and let all the stress out with your breath. Feel your belly get smaller as you breathe out.

Now take another deep breath, and count to five (in your head). Feel your belly rise again. You are taking in the air your body needs to feel good. And now let the breath and all the stress out again as your belly gets smaller.

Continue to take deep breaths to feed your body and breathe out to get rid of your stress. You may want to take at least five more breaths or until you feel calm.

You can use deep breathing whenever you feel stressed. It is also a nice way to relax before going to sleep.

Script 3 What's in a Raisin?

A Mini-Adventure in Mindfulness[2]

The Purpose

The purpose of this adventure is to do something ordinary with as much awareness as possible. Fully paying attention is called Mindfulness.

What You Need for this Adventure

- A small, individual size box of raisins

- A pen, pencil, and/or some art materials

- A notebook, a journal, or some paper

- A small plate

- Time

Setting the Scene

Set aside at least 15 or 20 minutes for this adventure when you know you will not be interrupted or distracted. Sit in a comfortable place with the instructions, your pen, and your notebook/journal nearby.

2   Diane Handlin Ph.D., Founder and Executive Director, Mindfulness-Based Stress Reduction Center of NJ, www.mindfulnessnj.com

Begin by very deliberately opening the box of raisins and putting a few of the raisins on the small plate. All the while imagine that you are from another place in the universe and have suddenly arrived here on earth. The objects on the plate are completely unknown to you. All you have are these instructions to guide you. Give yourself over to them.

So, let's get started. Pick up one of the objects from the plate and really focus full attention on it. See if you can drop away from all your associations and past ideas about this object. Feel what it feels like. Turn it around between your fingers. Put it in the palm of your hand and become aware of its color, size, and shape. Pick it up again and feel its temperature, its texture, its hardness, or softness.

Without doing anything, thoughts will occur quite naturally. All kinds of thoughts are possible. Some might be, "Why am I doing this," or "This is cool" or "This is stupid" or "I like this" or "I don't like this" or whatever thought might be there. Just for this short time, experiment with just noticing the thoughts for whatever they are without trying to change them or act on them. They are just thoughts and you can let them be there. Then bring your attention back to the raisin.

While being aware of the object in your palm, bring your palm up to your nose (also being aware of the movement of your arm as you do this) and smell the object. Let yourself become aware of what is happening inside your mouth as you smell the object -- noticing any tendency to want to put the object into your mouth automatically.

Taking your time, and when you are ready, put your full attention on the object in your mouth and bite it once. Carefully notice what is happening. Notice the taste. Notice the texture. Notice anything new going on in the rest of your mouth and any and all of the sensations there. Is something happening with your tongue? Are some things changing in your mouth and throat?

Now, slowly and mindfully, with as much sensory awareness as possible, gently chew the object, and, when you are ready, allow yourself to swallow it.

If you have time, take up your pen and note-book or journal and write about your experience. Don't worry about making full sentences or about grammar or spelling. Just let the words flow as they come up. You can use the following prompts to guide you, if you wish.

What were some of the things that you noticed when you looked at the raisin? Any smell? Any sense of texture? Any colors? Any likes or dislikes? Any thoughts just popping up?

What was it like to hold the raisin close to your nose? What was it like to put the raisin in your mouth? What was it like to swallow the raisin? Is this the way you usually eat?

Where was your attention during this activity? What did you notice about the object/raisin that you never noticed before?

Did you notice your attention wandering? What happened when it wandered? What would happen if you were to eat more like this?

If you wish, and you have art materials and time available, you might want to paint or draw the experience just allowing your inner creativity to flow and take over. If you're so inclined, you might even want to try writing a poem about it.

The History

The raisin has a history. It was once a grape that was part of a bunch of grapes. A farmer grew it in a certain kind of soil in a certain kind of weather with just the right amount of water. Someone picked the grape for you and worked hard to gather many, many grapes so they could be dried in the sun. In order to get the raisin to you, the raisin had to be put into a box with other raisins. Perhaps it was on an assembly line, and many people were involved in getting the raisin into its box and then packaging it. Each of these people also had a history. Maybe some of these people actually took a moment to feel something about the history of this object as it made its way toward you on its final journey.

Then, the raisins were shipped. Someone perhaps drove them by truck. After a long journey, they ended up in the store where you bought them. Someone put them on a shelf. Someone at a cash register took your money and checked you out. You brought the raisin home. Can you feel all of these connections and interactions that made it possible for you to get the raisin and be able to eat the raisin? We live in an interconnected world, but often are unaware of our interconnectedness.

Further Adventures in Mindful Eating

You might want to plan mindful eating activities with other foods. Also, you may want to plan to eat one snack a day mindfully, gradually working your way to being able to eat a meal mindfully. You may want to keep a mindful eating journal that can become a record of your adventures with various foods. Scientific research evidence indicates that mindful eating, if practiced regularly, helps people lose weight.

Script 4
Mindfullness Meditation
Body Scan

Mindfulness Meditation is a very special way of calming our bodies that has been used since ancient times (more than 2,600 years ago). It's a chance to journey into yourself as if meeting yourself for the first time in a new land. You will have a trustworthy friend with you along the way, and that friend is your attention. These words will be your map. To make this journey, you don't need to change a thing. All you'll need to do is to find a warm, comfortable place where you can lie down, if possible, or simply find a comfortable position which will allow you to pay attention in the most relaxed way.

So lying down on a mat or the floor (or on your bed if you prefer) carve out this special time just for you. Ask people not to interrupt you and put away any electronic devices for now. You can have them back again as soon as you have completed your journey. Congratulate yourself for taking the time to explore yourself in this way. This is a powerful tool for making you stronger. Some ancient cultures have practiced this throughout the ages. There is no right way to do this. However you are feeling is the way you should be feeling. Try to be patient with yourself and let the words lead your attention on this journey.

Now that you're lying down, or in a comfortable position, allow your eyes to close...Let your arms fall alongside your body with your palms up, keeping your feet uncrossed. See if you can feel your whole body at once while you are lying here right now. Can you experience how the floor, the mat, the rug or the bed are holding you up? Can you experience the power of gravity that is holding you on the earth as the earth is making its amazing journey through space? Let yourself sink a little more into whatever is supporting you, as you breathe in ... and then as you breathe out, resting a little more deeply ... into that support ... And now noticing that you are breathing ... Feeling how your chest and belly are moving as you breathe in and breathe out ... Each time you are breathing in, you are re-charging your energy, and helping your body grow ... .and when you are breathing out, visualizing yourself as clearing out what your body doesn't need anymore ... Breathing in ... Breathing out ... .being aware of yourself in this very special way ... .

Now, placing your hands on your belly, see if you can pretend that you have a balloon that you're filling with air in your belly ... .Breathing in deeply, feeling the balloon in your belly expanding ... and expanding ... And now breathing out and experiencing how the balloon deflates ... Now, again ... Breathing in ... feeling the balloon expanding ... breathing out, experiencing the balloon getting smaller and smaller... Noticing that you're breathing in new energy, bringing freshness to your body, and seeing if you can be sensitive enough to experience the special energy in each breath.

Some people call this feeling the Life Force in each breath ... it actually nourishes your life ... it keeps your body growing ... And, breathing in, you may actually be able to experience this energy going all the way down to the tips of your toes ... and to your fingertips, even into your fingernails, toenails, and even the roots of your hair ... It goes into every part of your body ... And, as you breathe out ... you're releasing, letting go, of what you no longer need ... It's as if your breath is clearing out your body, making room for new fresh energy to come in again on each next in-breath ... Breathing in ... and breathing out ... just being with your breath as if you are at the ocean and riding the waves of the breath ... just riding the waves of the breath ... with nothing else to do and no one else to be ... but just being your very special you, a magical, unique creature alive on this earth at this time ...

Your breath is a good friend ... It works all day for you, supporting your life and nourishing you. Every time you bring your attention to your breath, it gives you another opportunity, another moment to connect deeply with your strength and the miracle of your being alive ... So as you do this ancient body journey, allowing your attention to guide you through your body, with your breath as a kind of guide that keeps you on track or on the path, you can keep returning to a connection with your life force ...

If your mind starts to take you off somewhere else, simply acknowledging that, ... oh yes, there you are, old familiar thoughts ... .like an old friendly or unfriendly visitor, that I may want to visit or I may not ... simply putting them aside ... gently moving away from the thoughts for now (they can have you back again later if you choose to visit them) and recognizing that it is completely normal for your thoughts to be moving off in many different directions and that by becoming aware of this, you are developing a very special skill. Now you are returning to your guide, your attention, and your breath.

Continue to explore this country you are visiting, your own body, as if for the first time ... You can use your attention like a flashlight which you are shining on different parts of your body as we go along together ... So, letting the breath, the attention on the breath, simply move to the backdrop for a moment, and bringing the attention now to both of your feet ... .with your attention like the light from a flashlight on both feet ... And, noticing what you are feeling in your feet ... It may be a tingling, or they may feel warm or cool ... maybe they're covered by socks or shoes or maybe you've freed them up to feel the air around them ... .or you may feel nothing at all.

Whatever you are feeling is fine. Simply noticing it ... and now perhaps even imagining that your feet can breathe in as if they had a nose, and that they can breathe in fresh energy, and that as we breathe in, we can experience this special energy moving through all parts of both feet ... Your feet have an incredible number of nerve endings, but too often they're covered ... Right now, all you need is to feel yourself breathing into your feet, and now breathing out ... letting go of any old energy that's all used up.

Now, allowing your attention to move to the lower part of your body ... Becoming aware of your hips ... your belly, your lower back ... what are you feeling here? Do they feel cool or warm? Can you feel yourself lying down? Are you feeling your breath? The belly moving up and down as you did in the beginning ... Taking a deep breath in ... Letting your belly expand ... allowing the balloon to blow up in your belly ... blowing it up big ... and breathing new freshness into the lower part of your body ... and as you breathe out ... breathing out any tiredness that may be there.

Now, focusing on your back ... Sensing the bottom of your back, your middle back, your upper back ... noticing that there is a unique set of bones here that we call the spine ... .And there are nerves throughout the spine ... and they are protected as they branch out through the whole body ... so simply paying attention to any feelings you may have in any part of your back ... perhaps even feeling your rib cage moving with your breath ... and maybe even your heart beating ... . And noticing how your body actually moves to invite your breath ... and when you are breathing in, noticing once again that there is fresh energy in each in-breath that fills your lower, middle and upper back ... and now simply breathing out ... perhaps noticing the some differences in your experiencing of breathing in and out ... and now letting your back rest bit by bit more as you sink deeply into the mat or the bed or whatever it is upon which you are lying ... .

Now, coming back to the front of your body, letting your attention rest on your chest, and perhaps feeling your rib cage moving here as well. Noticing how the rib cage expands, opening, as it allows the lungs to hold more breath ... It's almost as if your ribs may be calling to you, "Come on now, breathe in more deeply, nourish your life ... we are making room for you."

So, breathing in, letting your breath move to the bottom of your lungs, now up the sides of your lungs, all the way to the top ... filling your lungs with energizing new breath ... And recognizing that your heart, which works all day long with your lungs, has even worked for you since before you were born ... Now noticing that each time you breathe in, your heart, together with your lungs, is transporting red blood cells that carry fresh energy to every tissue, cell, and organ in your body. And, as you breathe out, these two steadfast partners are getting rid of what's no longer needed ... .So now, attending to this incredible, unfailing activity, simply breathing in and breathing out ...

Allow your guide (your attention) to travel down both arms to both of your hands ... perhaps noticing the feelings you may have in your fingertips, and pausing for a moment to appreciate the miracle of having human hands ... all they allow you to do ... to write, to create, to play music, to experience pleasure, to express affection, to warn you of pain ... noticing if the fingertips may be moist or dry ... .or if your hands feel cool or warm and using the guiding flashlight of your attention, expanding that attention to both hands, breathing fresh energy into your hands and breathing out the old energy.

And now moving up both arms ... breathing into your arms and breathing out, and traveling on your journey to your shoulders and your neck ... and breathing into them ... and now breathing out ... nothing else to do ... no one else to be ... nowhere else to go ... but on this journey now ... .

Now arriving at your head ... are you able to feel your head touching whatever you are lying on ... can you sense your ears ... considering for a moment the miracle of your listening right now ... paying attention to hearing ... how does that happen ... what is your experience of hearing ... in between my words ... are you experiencing silence ... is silence really silence? What is your experience on this journey? And now your eyes, your nose, your cheeks, your mouth ... is your tongue resting on the roof of your mouth? What about your skull and the brain protected inside your skull ... not too many nerve endings here ... Can you invite your breath to move through all the parts of your head ... breathing in ... and breathing out ... .

If you care to, imagine that you have a small hole in the top of your head, like the blowhole of a whale. And, seeing if you can breathe in through this blowhole at the top of your head into your whole body, breathing fresh energy into your head, neck, shoulders, arms and hands, down through your whole back ... torso hips, thighs, knees, lower legs, ankles and feet. And now, when you arrive at the bottom of your feet, letting go of what's no longer needed, letting go of all effort ... if you care to, allow your breath to lead you all the way back up from the soles of your feet to the top of your head ... and perhaps even imagining that your breath is alive with a color that you like ... shining this beautiful colored light throughout all parts of your body ... and taking your time in doing this ... knowing that you are an incredibly miraculous being, right now, just as you are, without changing one thing! Knowing with all of your being that you are completely special, alive on this earth, and where there is no being like you ... .Congratulate yourself for getting to know yourself and care for yourself in this incredibly special way.

And now slowly, when you are ready, open your eyes, knowing you can always return to this journey again.

Putting it all together: Calming and facing fears.

Anxiety itself is not a problem, yet when it disrupts one's life with time-consuming, unnecessary routines (as in OCD), or it causes one to avoid desired activities, then anxiety becomes a problem. The purpose of calming strategies is to increase a sense of well-being, lower anxiety in general, and, specifically, lower anxiety enough so that individuals no longer need to avoid non-dangerous situations. Here are recommendations for using the calming tools previously discussed.

Active calming: All readers are encouraged to start an exercise program. This is cost-free; reduces anxiety; and can increase attention, memory, and learning, as well. Regular exercise should be a part of everyone's routine. Similarly, keeping busy with hobbies and other desirable activities can help reduce anxiety. These might include playing music, playing games, reading, and watching movies or shows. Such activities must be balanced with required activities like homework, coming to dinner, and getting to bed on time.

Quiet calming: Readers should experiment with progressive muscle relaxation, deep breathing, and mindfulness meditation to see which strategies are easier for them and which strategies reduce stress. These strategies should become part of a daily practice; for example, at bedtime, upon awaking, and, certainly, at anxious moments (before, during, and after facing a feared situation).

Using CBT to challenge anxious thinking is useful for all verbal children. Learning to combat the tendency to overestimate the frequency and consequences of future negative events is crucial to this process. Caregivers are encouraged to create the "Think Like a Scientist" cards for their children to use as a reminder of how to combat their particular worrisome thoughts.

Together, caregivers and children should create the "fear ladders" to identify situations to face in an effort to gradually overcome those fears. For young children (12 and under), or those less willing to face the feared situations on the ladder, external rewards should be identified to use as incentives for confronting a situation.

If the strategies and lifestyle changes described above do not sufficiently reduce anxiety, consider the use of neurofeedback and/or medication to further lower anxiety so that children are willing to face their fears. Although neurofeedback is quite safe in general, there is a cost and time commitment that may not make it everyone's first choice. Medications similarly may not be a first choice since they carry the risk of side effects. Medications could be considered if other strategies have failed to give desired results.

Remember, not all children will need all of these steps. Some children, like the girl with a phobia of bees and wasps described in chapter 7, may only need one tool to help face and overcome fears. Others, like the boy with social phobia described in chapter 8, may have more anxieties and need more tools to manage symptoms.

6 Adapting Treatment for Less Verbal Children with Autism

By "less verbal children," I refer to children with limited receptive language abilities who may not be able to comprehend verbal explanations. This is different than children with selective mutism who **do** understand and can use verbal language, but choose not to speak due to anxiety (see chapter 9).

Autistic children with limited receptive language may be referred to as having "classic" autism, labeled in the new DSM-5 diagnostic manual as, "autism spectrum disorder, Level 3." Verbal explanation is not adequate to help these children learn how to manage their anxiety.

In previous chapters, I spoke about teaching children about anxiety and the difference between true and false alarms. That is not as useful for children with limited receptive language. Moreover, less verbal children may not be able to report exactly what they fear; instead, those around them may have to detect the source of their fears based on observing the children.

Once the fear is identified, one can begin developing a fear ladder and reward the child for gradually climbing each step of the ladder by facing that fear. External rewards may be more useful for children who may not comprehend some of the naturally occurring rewards for facing fears (such as enjoying more activities, visiting new places, or having greater freedom).

Identifying their fears

Since less-verbal children cannot verbally tell you what makes them scared, those around them must observe which situations trigger anxiety responses. Anxiety response may mirror the "fight, flight or freeze response" discussed earlier. Children may show tantrum-like behavior (fight), run away (flight), or simply shut down and hide, refusing to talk, move, or interact (freeze). They may also show subtler signs of agitation: such as an increase in self-stimulatory behaviors, such as hand flapping, body rocking, or self-injurious behaviors.

In addition for looking at signs of anxiety and agitation, we can observe the triggers of these behaviors. Which situations, people, or activities are associated with upset or agitation? Which situations do the child actively avoid? For children who have more severe autism, consider the following common triggers (from Baker, 2008): demanding tasks, unexpected changes in routine, sensory overload (particular sights, sounds, smells, tastes or textures), or being denied access to something the child wants. In my book, *No More Meltdowns* (Baker, 2008), I outline a way of keeping track of challenging behaviors and these triggers in a diary format. In fact, there is an app called "No More Meltdowns"

(See the Apple App store, "No More Meltdowns" or visit www.symtrend.com/nmm) that will allow readers to keep track of challenging behaviors and triggers in real time on a mobile device. That data can then be uploaded to a website called www.symtrend.com/nmm which will analyze the data and help the user identify specific triggers associated with challenging behaviors.

Deciding whether to do exposure-based treatment or to simply change the environment

As you learn about what triggers your child's anxiety symptoms, you may decide that you can just let the child avoid the trigger or modify the trigger rather than helping him or her to face their fears. For example, many children are afraid of school fire alarms. It is possible to gradually expose children to such alarms to help them eventually habituate to the sound so that it does not provoke such anxiety and fear.

However, because fire alarms rarely occur, it may be easier and more efficient to simply excuse children from fire drills. The children could be removed from the building before activating such alarms.

In fact, whenever it is too difficult to teach a child to confront feared situations, it may be worth changing the situation instead of the child. These changes are called environmental supports and modifications.

Environmental supports for problems waiting, stopping something fun, or dealing with a change

Unexpected changes in routine are difficult for many individuals on the autism spectrum. Providing visual picture schedules ahead of time can help a youngster with autism prepare for what is ahead. If a regularly scheduled activity is going to be changed, you can show the change to the child ahead of time along with other activities to look forward to. For example, if outdoor recess is canceled, show the children that their favorite indoor games were put on the schedule in place of outdoor recess.

Use of visual schedules is also important when children with autism have perseverative interests. This means they want to do or play the same thing over and over again. For example, a child who loves trains may want to watch his train videos again and again. He may become anxious and angry if he is directed to stop watching to do another activity, or he has to wait a period of time before getting to his favorite interest. Having a clear schedule of when he can watch or return to the train video will help him wait and/or stop the activity to do another. A very useful app to help you create visual schedules for your child is called "visual scheduler." Not only can you import pictures into the schedule, you can also add video clips to show the child what to do at a certain part of the schedule.

Visual timers can also help when children have trouble waiting for favored items or activities. Children can become very anxious when they do not know when they will get what they want. Using a timer with a schedule can help. For example, if a child wants to play a video game, but he first needs to eat dinner, a parent can show on the schedule that dinner comes first, and then the video game. After that, the parent can set the timer for when dinner will be finished and video time begins. Visual timers allow kids who cannot tell time to see time past by using a shape or color that shrinks with the passage of time. Such timers are now readily available through an app called "Time Timer."

Modifying sensory challenges

There are two broad types of changes we can make to the sensory environment to reduce anxiety. One is to limit the amount of sensory input for those who get easily overwhelmed. The second is to increase the amount of sensory input for those who are easily bored and restless.

Examples of limiting sensory input include reducing sounds and sights and the amount of people interacting with the individual. Excusing children from fire drills is one example of this. Others include wearing noise cancelling headphones in loud environments or finding quiet rest areas when going to crowded areas like malls or parks.

For children who easily get bored and restless, provide frequent opportunities for comforting sensory input. These might include deep pressure massage, movement breaks in the form of physical exercise, or listening to music.

Modifying difficult demands

Children may be tremendously anxious about confronting a frustrating or difficult task. These include school work, dressing, cleaning up, or any task that may be challenging for that individual. A couple of general concepts can help lessen the anxiety associated with such demands.

First, just before presenting any difficult task, do easier ones that the individual can do successfully in order to build up confidence and a positive mood. This is referred to as the 80/20 rule (see Baker, 2008). Give 80% of the easy tasks before the 20% that are difficult.

Next, try to simplify the task for the child by modeling how to do the task. Help the child do it. For example, one can help children clean up by showing them where to put their things. One can help with school tasks by doing the first problems or tasks for them. You may prompt the child hand-over-hand to complete a task, such as drawing, cutting, pasting, or writing.

In addition, consider limiting the amount of tasks you first show the child. For example, if the child has five words to write or trace, show only one, then take a break. Come back later and do another. Seeing too much at once can raise anxiety.

Use visual schedules and incentives. Children may be less anxious about doing a task if they know a rewarding activity follows soon after. Use a "first/then" approach to display on a schedule each task to do followed by the reward. See example of "first/then" visual cue below.

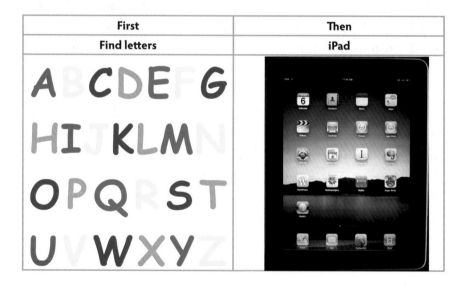

First	Then
Find letters	iPad

Set up a fear ladder when it is not sensible to avoid a situation

Some situations are not easy to modify or avoid. For example, a child with diabetes may require frequent checks of blood glucose level with a pinprick test. Just because he is fearful of the test does not excuse him from this life-sustaining routine.

With more verbal children, we create a fear ladder based on their self-report of the least to the most fearful situation. With less verbal children, we can use their behavior as a guide of how to set up the ladder. Shabani and Fisher (2006) used gradual exposure and rewards to help a youngster with autism and diabetes tolerate the pinprick blood tests.

They started by finding how close they could have the lancet (pinprick) near before he became agitated or pulled away. The closest they could come before he pulled away became the first rung on the fear ladder. They also used a preference test to determine what would be most rewarding for him and determined that cookies, popcorn, and soda were his most preferred items.

Over many trials, they slowly decreased the distance of the lancet to his finger and provided the edible rewards if he did not pull away for at least ten seconds. When they were only one cm (about ½ inch) away from his finger, they began every 10 trials or so to attempt a blood draw. This process was successful. The boy would allow his blood to be drawn daily without resistance.

Another common example of fear in less verbal children is related to separating from a parent. Separation anxiety makes it difficult for the child to attend school. Though I devote a later chapter to school refusal, I will explain here how to approach this issue with less verbal children.

Children may not trust that a parent will return after leaving. Try using a timer, first set to 10 seconds and tell the child you will return when the timer goes off. Leave the child with a trusted friend or relative and then return in 10 seconds. Then increase the time to 30 seconds. Again, leave and return when the timer goes off. Continue in this way until you build to a couple of minutes more, and eventually 30 minutes or an hour. You are trying to build the child's trust that you will return when the time is up. He or she may protest when you leave, but try to stick to the plan until the child seems calmer when you leave.

You can also reward the child for leaving a parent's side and entering school. One child loved karaoke music machines as a reward. The school arranged for a karaoke machine to be placed on the school bus, which got the child on the bus. The next day, the school arranged for the machine to be in front of the school when the bus arrived. On following days, the machine was placed in the classroom. The child had a picture schedule that showed when and where he would get the karaoke machine. This reward succeeded in getting him to school each day.

Explore tools to promote a relaxed state

Although guided verbal meditations may not be useful for children who cannot follow verbal instructions, similar approaches may indeed induce relaxation. Listening to music, calming voices on a meditation tape, or even simple instructions to breathe deeply may be effective in calming a youngster.

There are many books and articles on sensory strategies that may also help calm individuals on the spectrum (see Kranowitz, 2006). These approaches may be divided into two main categories: (1) those that help induce a state of alertness for children who are under-aroused, seek out stimulation, and often appear fidgety or hyper, and (2) those that help calm youngsters who are over-stimulated and may appear anxious or agitated.

Strategies that increase alertness typically involve movement. These may include:

- walking

- running

- jumping on a trampoline

- fast rocking or swinging

- bouncing on a therapy ball

- mini-jobs like stacking books or furniture

- compression movements like wall pushups or pushing hands together

- listening or dancing to fast music

Calming strategies for those who are overaroused may include:

- slow rocking in a rocking chair

- deep pressure massage or compression (such as pushing a large pillow on the child from the neck down to mimic a feeling of being swaddled)

- wrap up snugly in a blanket or towel

- create a comfortable quiet area away from noise and filled with pillows and blankets

- mouth relaxers like sucking candies or chewing on gum or a straw

- squeezing a foam ball or other soft toy

- listening to slow and rhythmic music

- watching slow visual patterns like a lava lamp or relaxing, moving designs on a IPad

These techniques can be scheduled throughout the day to maintain a relaxed state. Children and teens can also use these just before and after facing a feared situation. This helps the youngster cope better.

If these relaxation strategies, along with environmental modifications and/or gradual exposure to feared situations fail to work, and the youngster is unable to function in school or at home, one might consider adding neurofeedback or medications to further reduce anxiety.

7 Simple Phobia

Ellie was a relatively typical nine-year-old afraid of stinging insects, particularly bees and wasps. Other than this fear, she was not a particularly anxious child. She was bright, outgoing, and able to make friends. However, she often missed out on outside play with others during the summer months because she was afraid of being stung. She had never been stung, but had seen others stung. She also believed it was very dangerous. She had heard some people have allergies and could go into anaphylactic shock. People could even die from a sting! Her parents had taken her to an allergist who confirmed that Ellie was **not** allergic to insect bites.

Winning Ellie over to the idea of working on her fear was relatively easy, as she was aware of her strong friendships and understood how the fear left her out of social events.

We began treating Ellie by explaining how anxiety works. We described the difference between true and false alarms. Ellie learned that her alarm reaction caused real internal physical symptoms, such as a rapid heartbeat and tension. However, the external danger was not as real as she anticipated. Ellie's reaction was explained as a false alarm, because the probability of getting stung was lower than she expected, and the consequence of getting stung was much less severe than she thought.

The goal of treatment was not to eradicate her fear, as some caution makes sense. None of us need to disrupt a wasps' nest and be on the receiving end of numerous stings. However, the goal was to take realistic precautions rather than avoid being outdoors with her friends.

We used the "Think Like a Scientist" strategy, researching the probability and danger of being stung. In collecting factual information, it became clear that wasps and bees generally are not aggressive when away from their nests. They are not likely to sting unless threatened by being swatted, hit, or stepped on. In addition, though a sting can cause pain, redness, and swelling, it is not dangerous if one does not have an allergy. As the allergist confirmed, Ellie was not allergic. We also reviewed the reasonable precautions Ellie could take to reduce the chances of being stung. See the summary of Ellie's "Think Like a Scientist" strategy.

We used this summary to help motivate Ellie to start facing her fears. We created a fear ladder for spending increasing time outside during the summer, along with

Think Like a Scientist

Feared situation	Anxious thought	Realistic outcome
Getting stung by a bee or wasp	Being outdoors in the summer makes it likely to be stung	Bees and wasps are not aggressive away from nests. Not likely to sting unless swatted, hit, or stepped on. If I avoid nests, wear shoes when walking in leaves, and do not swat, I am not likely to be stung. I can also cover up food or stay away from garbage cans where those insects gather.
	Getting stung really hurts and maybe I could even die	It is not possible for me to die because I am not allergic. I can reduce the pain by immediately flicking or taking out the stinger to limit the venom and apply ice for the swelling. I have had injections before and stings are actually less painful.

a reward menu for each step confronted (as shown below). High on the ladder was staying outside when a bee or other stinging insect was visible. Facing this situation earned Ellie the largest reward. We reminded her before she went out, that when she did see a stinging insect, if she backed away slowly, and did not swat at it, she was not likely to be stung.

Ellie's Fear Ladder and Reward Menu

Situation	Reward menu
Stay outside in backyard for 5 minutes	$1, or a sweet treat
Stay outside in backyard for 10 minutes	$2, or 2 sweet treats
Stay outside in backyard for over 20 minutes	$5, or 3 treats, or trip to ice cream parlor
Stay outside in park for 10 minutes	$3, or 3 sweet treats
Stay outside in park for over 20 minutes	$7, or 4 treats, or trip to ice cream parlor
Stay out for at least 3 more minutes when a bee or wasp is visible	$10, or two outings to ice cream parlor, or a sleepover

Though we could have added situations to Ellie's fear ladder, it was not necessary. After she stayed out twice when a bee was visible and nothing bad happened, she no longer avoided going outside. She continued to take precautions: covering up food outside as well as avoiding trash cans and any signs of nest areas.

8 Social Anxiety

Kyle was a 12-year-old in the 6th grade. He was diagnosed with Aspergers's syndrome (AS) and social phobia. Although he had made some friends in elementary school, he no longer reached out to them in middle school. Kyle sat alone at lunch and also kept to himself in class. When his mother encouraged him to call his friends, Kyle refused. Like many children with AS, he was not only anxious about connecting with peers, but (according to his parents and the staff at his previous elementary school) he did not really know how.

Historically Kyle had difficulty starting and maintaining conversations, especially on topics other than his special interest, Minecraft. For much of the first month of 6th grade, he did not socialize with any peers except online when playing his favorite video game.

Kyle was a good student, but the transition to middle school was hard. He was given more homework and longer term projects. He was also supposed to work at a faster pace. After meeting with the school support team, his parents and the staff agreed that his anxiety about school work and interacting with others had worsened.

The school agreed to provide Kyle with a social skills group (facilitated by me) with high-functioning, bright peers who also had both social anxiety and skill challenges. The school also provided help organizing his homework in a study skills class. Kyle received access to a counselor who could help him problem-solve if he was having difficulty in a class and needed to talk with a teacher.

The homework help seemed to lower Kyle's anxiety about getting his work done, yet he continued to resist reaching out to peers. In the first couple of weeks of the social skills group, Kyle was very quiet. With my help facilitating group conversation, he learned some key skills to start and maintain conversations (see "Summary of Starting and Maintaining Conversations" in Baker, 2001).

Kyle practiced talking with his peers in the school social group and learning about their shared interests. His parents had copies of his skill sheets, and they practiced with him over dinner at home. He, as well as the other boys, also learned about their many strengths and talents.

Most boys had great factual knowledge of many subject areas, especially those focused around preferred interests, such as video gaming. They appreciated their

Summary of Conversation Skills

Talking with people you know	
Guess what	(something you did)
Past:	How was your_____? (week, week-end, day, vacation)
Present:	What are you _____? (doing, reading, eating, playing)
Future:	What are you going to do __? (after school, this weekend, over vacation)
Shared Interests:	Did you _____? (sport, class, games they play)
Other's interest:	How is _____? (sport, class, pet, hobby, job)
How is _____?	(sport, class, pet, hobby, job)
Keep Conversations Going	
Ask	**Tell**
Who?	I like _____
What?	I also _____
When?	I never _____
Where?	My _____
Why?	
How?	
What else?	
Getting to Know New People	
Name::	What's your name? Mine is _____.
Age::	How old are you? I am _____.
Fun::	What do you like to do for fun? TV, movies, books, places they like to go, games, sports, food.
School:	What school do they go to? Grade, subjects, teachers
Family:	Do you have any brothers or sisters? Pets?

mutual talents, and from this position of strength, they began to identify a smaller number of challenges, such as socializing with others.

Not accidentally, the boys in the group all shared an interest in video games, including Minecraft. After three weeks, I had the boys exchange their contact information and encouraged them to get together around shared interests. Kyle was open to the idea but did not reach out at first.

During the next sessions, I began explaining to the boys how anxiety works. All of us have both true and false alarms. The boys shared some of their current or past false alarms, from social fears to anxiety about grades, making mistakes, and fears of spiders and other animals. Kyle seemed visibly relieved to see that everyone had fears like him. I encouraged the boys to think about small steps they could take to face their fears and discover that these were just false alarms. I taught them about the problems of overestimating the likelihood and consequences of negative events.

For Kyle, this was about assuming that other kids would not like him, would reject invitations to get together, and that he would not know what to do or say if kids did hang out with him. We reviewed the conversation skills he had learned so that he could see that he now knew what to say.

He would have plenty to do if he got together with those who had similar interests. The other boys in the group all volunteered that they would like to get together with him and play video games. The stage was now set to help Kyle connect with peers outside of school.

Kyle created a fear ladder from least to most fearful, so he could gradually face the fear of socially connecting with peers. First, he decided that responding to a peer's phone call or text would be easier than making a call himself. I encouraged the other boys to reach out to Kyle. He only needed to respond to them. If the group accomplished this, we would celebrate with cupcakes the next session.

I told the parents about the plan, and during the next week, Kyle successfully responded to a call from one of his peers. Though they did not get together, Kyle and his peer discussed plans to have a get-together.

At the next group meeting, Kyle beamed, as he and the other boys were heroes because they were responsible for everyone getting cupcakes. Kyle made plans to respond to his peers again the following week. One of the boys planned a get-together with Kyle, but then did not show up. That boy forgot to call Kyle and tell him that he had to reschedule.

I explained to Kyle that the other boy was not rejecting him and that he simply forgets things sometimes. Kyle was able to call him when he did not show up, and they rescheduled for the next day. They successfully met and played video games.

We celebrated again at the next group session. Kyle felt very proud of himself. He was willing to call some of the other boys in the group who had indicated that they wanted a get-together. That week happened to be a vacation week, and Kyle ended up having three get-togethers, including seeing one of his old friends.

Kyle had apparently become confident enough to reach out to his old friends. He realized they had not rejected him, but had pulled away because Kyle had been less responsive in the beginning of the year. This is a very important lesson.

Frequently those with social phobia assume others do not like them when really it's the others who think the individual with social phobia does not like them. Kyle began to see how his reticence made others think that he was not interested, when in fact, he was just fearful.

As the group continued through the year, other fears emerged for Kyle, such as speaking in front of the class. His new-found confidence from get-togethers helped him want to tackle these fears, as well.

In addition to challenging his thoughts about what others might think if he said something silly in front of his class, Kyle learned a couple of other relaxation techniques like deep breathing. He began an aerobic exercise program at home (stationary bike). The exercise and deep breathing proved crucial in helping Kyle improve his confidence and mood to the point where he began to answer questions in class, make comments, and eventually present an oral report.

9 Selective Mutism

Katie was a 5-year-old kindergartner with selective mutism, but no known developmental delays, and an average to above average IQ. Katie would not talk in front of anyone other than her family and some very close friends. In school she would not speak to peers or teachers.

She had similar issues in a preschool setting, and her parents had hoped she would grow out of it. For the first two months of kindergarten, however, she refused to speak in school.

Katie's mother had told me that she, too, had had similar anxiety as a child and continued to feel social anxiety as an adult. Nevertheless, mom had learned to face her fears enough to work, marry, and make friends, but she had never told her daughter about her own anxiety. Mom's story of how she overcame her own anxiety would become a very powerful tool in helping Katie.

To begin treatment, we needed to learn all of Katie's talents and strengths. These included her strong pre-academic skills (she could sound out words and do simple addition), her excellent gymnastic ability, and happy demeanor at home. Although Katie would not speak to me, she listened carefully as we reviewed her strengths.

We then discussed her challenge of not talking in school and how that could make it hard for folks to know about her talents. I explained that not talking can happen when people feel scared. I then educated her about our alarm system and false alarms. Here is what I said:

All of us have an alarm in our brains that tell us when things are scary or dangerous. When our alarm goes off, our heart beats quickly. We feel tense, and we want to get away from what scares us.

Sometimes, we have true alarms and sometimes we have false alarms. True alarms are when there really is something dangerous, like a car that may hit us. False alarms are when we are afraid, but there really is no danger, like talking in front of your friends or a really nice teacher.

Some people have really sensitive alarm systems that go off all the time. You might have one of those. Mommy does, too. Mommy said she was also really scared to talk to people when she was little. But her mommy taught her that it was a false alarm. Even though it feels scary, nothing bad will happen if she talks in front of people. So mommy tried it, and now she is able to talk to all kinds of people. Her alarm still goes off and she feels nervous, but she does not let that stop her from being brave and talking to others.

We want you to be like mommy and find out that nothing bad will happen if you talk to others in school. We know that's really scary for you, so we do not want to have you do it all at once. We can start with easier steps like just nodding "yes" or "no," or whispering only to people you know well, like your best friend in school. And because this is hard to do, we want to give you rewards for trying it. You can earn lollipops and other treats that you and mommy decide on.

We then showed Katie the Fear Scale and asked her to rate how scary different situations were. Based on that, we created the following fear ladder from least to most fearful.

Katie's Fear Ladder and Reward Menu

Situation	Points
Nod "yes" or "no"	1
Whisper to best friend who can then tell others what she said	2
Whisper to other peers or teacher	3
Talk in louder voice to peers or teacher	4
Talk to any classroom visitors	5

3 points earns a candy in school.

All points are added at home each day for a longer term reward like special purchases or privileges (e.g., 15 points earned her a new stuffed animal).

Katie was able to earn points quickly for nodding, something she had already been able to do at times. Yet, we wanted to start with success. As long as she nodded at least three times per day in response to her teacher, she received her candy. The family and I highly praised Katie for facing her fear and responding to her teacher.

To help her with the next step of talking through her best friend, we set up get-togethers with this friend on the Sunday night before the beginning of the school week and several times during the weeknights. The added comfort of these get-togethers allowed Katie to begin to talk with her friend in school, and she eventually asked her friend to tell her teacher or other peers what she needed.

Whenever the teacher pushed too hard to encourage her to talk, Katie would slip back and respond less. It was crucial that Katie be encouraged and rewarded, but not pressured in any negative way, as that added to her discomfort and fear.

After a month of treatment, Katie continued to respond with non-verbal gestures and by whispering though her friend. She had not yet spoken directly to the teacher or other peers. Sometimes we can break the ice of talking to a new person by first giving the new person an audio recording of the child.

We asked Katie if she would let us give a recording of her voice to the teacher. Katie selected a recording of her doing a pretend play with her stuffed animals at home. The teacher told Katie that it was a wonderful play, and she really enjoyed hearing it. Her teacher did not say anything else about the sound of Katie's voice, as she did not want to pressure her to talk. Soon after this, Katie whispered to the teacher, and then to her peers.

We were now about three months into treatment. Things had gone well, with some predictable setbacks. Generally, Mondays and any days after vacations were the most difficult, because Katie had been out of practice talking in school. Once back, she would begin talking (although in a whisper) to others once again. Her ratings of how fearful she was went from 5s to 3s or 2s.

The last struggle was to get Katie to raise her voice volume. I spoke with her mom about starting Katie on an exercise program (in addition to her weekly gymnastics). She began taking walks with her mother before school, including a walk/run to school on many days. In addition, her mom started implementing a combination of deep breathing and mindfulness meditation at bedtime to help them both relax. With these additional tools, Katie's confidence improved, and she began raising her volume in school.

Katie received copious praise from her parents, teachers, and me and was feeling very good about her accomplishments. As school let out for summer, there was concern that she may slip back. We tried to extend the reward system to a day camp, yet she requested not to use it as she did not need it.

She was right; without any intervention, she was able to talk in camp to others. Moreover, she extended her gains to school the next year. From time to time, she had other anxieties, such as sleeping away from home, yet mom and Katie now had the tools to face those fears, as well.

10 Separation Anxiety and School Refusal

Though separation anxiety and school refusal often co-exist in younger kids, there are many older children who do not have problems separating from their parents, yet continue to demonstrate a pattern of school refusal.

Here are two cases: a 4-year-old, Jonathon, with separation anxiety and school refusal; and a 15-year-old girl, Mandy, with school refusal but without separation issues.

Jonathon

Jonathon was 4-year-old boy with some attentional challenges and was having a difficult time separating from his mother to go to preschool. The school tried to get her to leave him and let him cry it out. With most young children, parents can leave them at school. They will cry briefly, and within some minutes, they will calm.

Over the course of a couple of weeks or so, most kids get accustomed to a new school, and all is well. Not the case with Jonathon. When his parents tried to leave him, his response was so intense that he would fight his teachers, scream, and run back to his parents unless he was restrained. His tantrum would last the better part of the day if his mom left him.

Mom indicated that he also had similar separation issues at home, refusing to go to a friend's house by himself and tantrumming if his parents went out for the evening and left him with a baby sitter. In addition, he slept in his parents' bed at night because he did not like to be alone in his bed.

Treatment focused on three parts: helping Jonathon understand his fear as a false alarm, setting up a fear ladder for separating from his parents to attend preschool, and eventually facing the fear of sleeping in his own bed.

To help Jonathon understand his fears, I said many of the same things I said to Katie in the previous chapter:

All of us have an alarm in our brains that tells us when things are scary or dangerous. When our alarm goes off, our heart beats quickly, we feel scared, and we want to be near our parents. Sometimes, we have true alarms and sometimes we have false alarms. True alarms are when there really is something dangerous, like a car that may hit us.

False alarms are when we are afraid, but there really is no danger, such as when mommy or daddy leaves you at a nice school for just a little while. They always come back, so there really is no danger. But, your alarm system may go off, and you think it is dangerous even though it's not.

The only way to find out it really is a false alarm is to try being without mommy and daddy for short amounts of time and then find out that all is okay. Since that is hard to do, we only want you to try being away from them for really short amounts of time and give you rewards for trying it.

We then showed Jonathon a visual timer (from an app called Visual Timer). He could see the time pass using either a shrinking shape or an hour glass. We set the timer for 15 seconds so he could see how long that was. Then we set it for 1 minute, then 2.

We asked him how long he thought he could try being away from mommy before she came back into the room. We started with 1 minute, then 2, then 3. Then we began to double the time to 6 minutes and eventually got all the way to 12.

Next, we suggested he try this at the school. Start with 1 minute, then 2, then 3, then 6, then 12. We said for each time period he went without mommy in the preschool room, he could get a small candy of his choice. He successfully met these challenges because the time frame was short.

In our subsequent therapy sessions, we tried to extend the time to 24 minutes (and eventually 48 minutes) during which time we talked about things he could do, instead of thinking about mommy, because she would return when the timer was up.

If he began to become agitated, we described it as a false alarm. However, we let mommy return as he requested and announced how long he had gone, and then challenging him to see how long he could do it the next time. We let Jonathon stay in control, but continued to challenge him with how long he could last, laying on the praise and rewards for each period he could tolerate.

After 3 sessions, Jonathon got up to an hour. We transferred this to the school setting. In a typical school morning, Mom would leave him at the school for 5 minutes, then 10, then 15, then 30, then 60. Each time, she would return, reward him with a treat, praise him, and redirect him to the timer to see if he could do it again.

The teacher talked with Jonathon about what he could do to make it easier to wait: participating in circle time, drawing, playing, and other activities. There were times when he became agitated and was given the option to call mom in earlier, but was reminded he only got the reward if he could wait it out and discover it was a false alarm. After two weeks, with some anxious moments where he asked for mom's return earlier than hoped, he was able to extend the wait for the entire three-hour (half-day) preschool.

We now turned our attention to bedtime by using a very similar approach with a timer. We asked Jonathon to wait for progressively longer periods before mom would return to the room. The procedure involved a consistent bedtime ritual, such as the parents reading a story, comforting Jonathon briefly, and then telling him they would return in 5 minutes to check on him.

Upon checking, they would praise him, comfort him briefly, and then tell him to check the timer and they would return in 10 minutes. Jonathon's parents would continue this procedure until he fell asleep while they were out of the room.

Jonathon's goal was to learn to fall asleep on his own. The problem with children only falling asleep in the presence of their parents is that they can quickly become dependent on their parents' presence. Using progressive waiting to help children sleep in their own bed was originally described by Ferber (1985, 2006) and is described in greater detail in my book *No More Meltdowns* (Baker, 2008).

To help Jonathon relax at bedtime, and at times when neither parent was in his room, they also gave him a guided meditation for children they found on an app of meditations. They recorded it on an iPod so that he could hear it whenever he needed.

Establishing a pattern of falling and staying asleep in his bed took longer to accomplish with Jonathan, partly because, if he woke in the middle of the night, his parents were asked to return him to bed and start the timer again. As you can imagine, this was exhausting, and the parents often let Jonathon just stay in their bed if he awoke in the middle of the night.

As time went on, they compromised and put a blow up mattress in their bedroom if he entered their bedroom in the middle of the night. This also stalled progress as he often looked forward to coming in to their room at night.

Eventually, during a vacation week, his parents began returning Jonathon to his room, comforting briefly, and then leaving him with the timer to let him know when they would return again to check on him. Tackling a job like this was best done during a period when parents were off from work so they could afford to do the tiring work of taking him back to his bed. As long as the parents consistently returned Jonathon to his bed, he was able to fall back asleep on his own.

Mandy

Mandy was a 15-year-old girl who was to attend a special education school for the first time. She had a long history of school refusal in her regular public school and had been placed out-of-district with the hope she would attend a school that was better matched for her learning and emotional needs.

Mandy had been diagnosed with an autism spectrum disorder, attention deficit hyperactivity disorder-combined type, anxiety disorder, and several learning disabilities. She was also taking Wellbutrin® and Zoloft® to help manage her symptoms.

The special education school referred her to us for treatment because she was not regularly attending school. Her parents reported that they were unable to get her to follow a routine in which she would dress, take care of basic hygiene, and get to school. In addition, when she refused to go to school or said she was too ill, she spent the day playing video games.

Treatment involved several steps:

- individual therapy to help establish Mandy's willingness to address the school refusal

- family therapy to help structure morning routines, getting Mandy to school, as well as limiting screen time if she did not go to school.

- creating a fear ladder and incentive program to help her attend school

To begin, we spoke with Mandy about her strengths and her goals for the future. Despite a challenging school history, her testing revealed that she was a bright young lady, who, with some academic supports for writing, could be quite successful. We explained she was now slotted to go to a school that was able to provide her with the right supports for success if she could overcome her anxiety about attending.

We then explained about true versus false alarms, helping her to consider that her school refusal was based on a false alarm. The danger in school was now quite unlikely given the supports it provided. She learned about the specific academic and peer supports available which helped challenge some unrealistic (but understandable) fears she had about possible social and academic problems.

In a meeting with Mandy and her parents, we developed a fear ladder and an incentive program to reward her for following an evening hygiene routine, a morning routine to get ready for school, an increasing cooperation with travel to school, and, finally, increasing amounts of time remaining in school for the day. The fear ladder we created for Mandy is shown below.

Mandy's Fear Ladder and Reward Program

Feared Situation	Reward (Minutes of Screen Time)
Completion of evening hygiene	10
Completion of morning routine	10
Get on bus	20
Get in car and be driven to school	10
Get out of car at school	10
Enter school building	10
Remain at school for 15 minutes	20
Remain in school for one full period	20
Remain in school for half-day	30
Remain in school for the full day	60
Total:	

Working with her parents, we helped them to follow through with helping her through the evening and morning routines, getting to school, and dealing with any refusals. For example, if she refused to go to school claiming she was sick, she had to go to the doctor rather than stay home. If she stayed home, she was not allowed screen time. Screen time was earned for efforts to get to school.

Some of Mandy's hygiene issues were not just related to her refusal to go to school. She had sensory issues around use of hair removal products and sensitivity to water in the shower. She disliked the feel of water hitting her body in the shower. By bathing in the tub instead of the shower, doing it in the evening, using bubble bath, and listening to music, Mandy was able to overcome her discomfort. We were also able to find a hair removal product that she could tolerate.

After a few days, Mandy made it to the school. On that day, she had planned to just stay for 15 minutes but ended up staying the entire day. As she learned that school was not as uncomfortable as she anticipated, Mandy was more willing to attend in subsequent days. Though she threatened not to go at times, with reminders of her screen time earnings, Mandy went, sometimes a few minutes late.

The school worked to help facilitate new friendships, identified an appropriate support group, and encouraged the girls to get together. Her friendships became another motivation for her to attend school. When Mandy discovered that one of her friends rode the same bus, Mandy began to consistently make the bus in the morning.

11 Panic Disorder

Arlene was 13 years old when she described her first panic attack. It occurred after her family dropped off her father at the airport for a business trip. She does not recall worrying that something would happen to him, but remembers being in the car coming home from the airport when a wave of panic hit her. She remembers her heart beating out of her chest, feeling dizzy and slightly nauseous.

When Arlene was younger, her parents said that she had some strong separation anxiety in preschool and a little into kindergarten. She also had some transient fears of neighborhood pets, and a strong disgust reaction to vomit with subsequent avoidance of anyone reporting feelings of nausea.

After this first panic attack, Arlene feared having the reaction again, particularly in the car where it first occurred. During two subsequent attacks, one in the car and one in gym class at school, her parents brought her to an urgent care center to make sure there was nothing wrong with her heart or any other physical ailment. All medical tests were normal. Her doctors referred Arlene for psychiatric treatment, where she was diagnosed with panic disorder. The psychiatrist referred her to us for treatment before considering a trial of medication.

As a result of her previous panic attacks, Arlene was reluctant to ride in her mom's car or go to gym class because she feared having another attack. We began treatment by educating her about panic disorder and the body's alarm system. She learned that her panic attacks were her body's very strong alarm reaction. Although the attacks caused real symptoms, they did not pose a real threat to her. We framed them as false alarms.

We explained that the purpose of treatment was not necessarily to rid her of the panic attacks, but to be able to better tolerate them and not go to great lengths to avoid places where she previously had those attacks.

It was the avoidance, we stressed, that created the real problem. The attacks themselves never lasted for more than 10-15 minutes and were not physically harmful to her. The analogy we used to describe her surge of anxiety was the idea of an ocean wave.

Her panic came on gradually and then surged, but like a wave, it soon dissipated. We asked if we could help her ride it out so that she could participate fully in school and car rides and not be imprisoned by the fear of another attack.

To help her face the symptoms of these panic attacks, we first employed the "Think Like a Scientist" strategy. Arlene continued to feel that it was possible for her to become physically ill from an attack: from a heart problem, fainting, or vomiting.

We reminded her that the doctor said that she was healthy, with no heart problems, and, despite some dizziness and nausea, she had never fainted or threw up from a panic attack.

These symptoms were quite literally an autonomic activity of her nervous system that readied her for fight or flight. Another fear was that she would be embarrassed in front of others because they might see her panicking and wonder what was wrong with her. We explained that despite her very strong internal feelings, it was not easy for others to see that she was having an attack.

We also gave her some ready-made explanations and excuses if she needed to find a safe place when in public. For example, Arlene could tell people she had a stomachache and excuse herself to the bathroom. If she were in a car, she could just say she had a little motion sickness and needed to take some breaths or get some air. A summary of her "Think Like a Scientist" strategy is shown below.

In addition to combating her worrisome thoughts, we wanted Arlene to gradually face the fear of her physical panic symptoms and see that they are soon over and do not harm her. We discussed a variety of activities that might bring about symptoms of panic, such as rapid heartbeat, dizziness, or mild nausea. Some of these activities included quickly running up stairs, hyperventilating into a paper bag, taking rapid deep breaths for increasing amounts of time, or spinning in circles until mildly dizzy or nauseous.

Arlene's Think Like a Scientist Summary

Feared situation	Anxious thought	Realistic outcome
Panic attack	It may be related to heart problems, cause fainting or vomiting	MD said I am healthy, no heart problems and I never have fainted or vomited. Even if I did, I could explain it as feeling sick that day. The attack will be over within 15 minutes.
Panic in front of peers	They notice and think I am crazy	Despite the strong internal sensations, it is hard to see from the outside. I can also say I have a stomachache or motion sickness if I need to excuse myself to another place for a moment.

Our goal was to habituate Arlene to some of these physical symptoms. We set up a fear ladder that included these activities along with attending gym and riding in mom's car (see below):

Arlene had made it through her fear ladder after about a month of weekly sessions. We assigned her the situations listed on her fear ladder as homework. Her fear level for each situation was consistently at a 1 or 2. However, she had two additional panic attacks during this time: one just before school, and another riding home from school in the car.

Arelene's Fear Ladder

Situations	Fear level 1-5
Run up and down the stairs for 30-60 seconds	2
Breathe rapidly or breathe in and out of a paper bag for 15 second increments. Try to extend to 4 increments.	3
Spin around in circles until mildly dizzy or nauseous	3
Attend gym and excuse self to bathroom to "try out" escape route	4
Ride in mom's car and request a brief break for motion sickness to "try out" escape route	4

Although Arlene knew it was not harmful, and would not avoid going to school or the car, she nevertheless found it quite uncomfortable. She wanted to reduce the frequency of panic attacks.

We began a slow jogging program to provide aerobic exercise without a rapid heartbeat. In addition, Arlene explored a variety of meditation apps and settled on a couple of meditations she liked. She used them before bed and also began to use them whenever she felt some-what anxious during the day, focusing on taking slow, deep breaths.

These coping tools were moderately effective. Ar-lene reduced the number of panic attacks to one per month. More importantly, she did not avoid situations for fear of having another attack. However, after three months, she opted to try an antidepressant medication as an additional tool to dampen the likelihood of having more panic attacks.

After several weeks on the medication, Arlene had noticeably fewer panic attacks, about one every two months. Though she was not able to entirely rid herself of the panic, she did learn to cope with it, and she did not avoid situations for fear of having an attack. Arlene knew she could go to a quieter place to ride it out if necessary, and, although inconvenient, she knew it would not harm her.

12 Obsessive Compulsive Disorder

I treated Chris between the ages of 7 and 16 years. In addition to having some learning challenges, he had a history of compulsive hand washing.

When I met Chris at age 7, he had been washing his hands more than 25 times per day to the point where his hands would crack and occasionally bleed. He had numerous obsessive fears about getting sick from others' germs and avoiding shaking hands, touching door knobs, touching any items belonging to others, and touching sink faucets with his bare hands (he used a paper towel). His hand washing not only interfered with his schooling, as he left the class frequently to wash, but it was also causing potential health issues by creating open wounds on his hands.

In meeting with Chris, it was clear that a large part of his stress was related to school demands. He was frequently frustrated, refused to do work, and then was reprimanded by his teachers for not working. In response to being punished with the loss of recess for not doing work, he sometimes yelled at the teacher, threw chairs, or threatened to push her.

Chris had been suspended several times, each time returning (with a couple of good days) before he once again had conflicts with his teacher. What was most interesting is that his hand washing had only begun upon entering first grade with its increasing academic demands.

Before directly addressing his hand washing, we decided to try to lessen the academic frustrations and power struggles in school that increased his stress and anxiety level. We met with his school and developed a behavior plan to modify work demands in line with his abilities, provided extra help from a resource room in school, and reduced homework demands.

Chris learned that he could ask for help or a break without being punished for not completing his work. After his teacher allowed him to take breaks without completing his work, Chris reported that he felt better in school.

By this point, his hand washing dropped to roughly 10 times-per-day, a significant reduction. Reducing his overall anxiety had a direct impact on his fear of germs and on his need to wash. However, his fears and washing were still an issue that needed to be addressed.

We began by getting Chris on board with why it might be important to work on this. Now that school was going better, we could highlight his achievements and talk about how the washing sometimes interfered with learning and caused potential health challenges due to cracked hands.

We described how we all have an internal "alarm" system and that there are true and false alarms. We then explained what the term Obsessive Compulsive Disorder (OCD) meant, describing how people may have scary thoughts that repeat over-and-over in their heads creating a false alarm. Some people then perform some repetitive behavior (a compulsion) to stop that scary feeling. We explained that he has obsessions about germs that cause false alarms, and those false alarms cause him to wash more than necessary to get rid of that bad feeling.

We talked about the part of his brain that tells him to fear germs as the "OCD" part of his brain. Borrowing from Dawn Huebner (2007) in her book for kids about OCD, we described the OCD part of his brain as a big bully lying about the dangers of germs and forcing him to do things like wash all the time. We encouraged Chris to not let the bully control him.

To help him see that his fears were really false alarms, we created a "Think Like a Scientist" worksheet to counter his fearful thoughts. Specifically, he was afraid that by touching public property, door handles, or others' pencils or belongings, he would pick up a germ that would get him very sick unless he could immediately wash his hands.

Chris also felt that he needed to use very hot water and wash several times to insure the germs were off of him. He also used alcohol-based sanitizers throughout the day for germs he got from other places. We explained that, although germs do exist and can spread infectious disease, his best defense is intact skin. Broken skin can allow germs to enter the body. To insure unbroken skin, he needed to be very picky about the times he washed so as to reduce the frequency. Specifically, Chris learned that these are the only necessary times to wash (and to wash only once):

- Before and after preparing food, especially when handling raw meat and poultry

- Before eating or preparing food, or after touching any raw meat, poultry or eggs

- Before and after touching an open wound

- Before or after touching a sick person

- Before inserting contact lenses

- After using the toilet

- After touching an animal

- After blowing your nose or coughing/sneezing into your hands

- After handling garbage or waste

We explained to Chris that washing more than once in these situations only increased the chance of breaking his skin, making him more prone to germs entering his body. We also discussed that if germs were on his hands, but he did not rub his eyes, or put his fingers in his mouth, he would keep those germs out of his body.

Then we discussed how dangerous it would be if he did get a germ inside his body. Lethal germs are generally not found in any of the places he ventured. The only germs Chris was likely to encounter were those related to the common cold virus, stomach or flu virus, or

Chris's Think Like a Scientist Summary

Feared situation	Anxious thought	Realistic outcome
Touching germs	I will get a lethal disease.	I have skin that will protect me if I leave it intact and do not over-wash or crack the skin. Germs I encounter are not lethal and can only cause minor, treatable illnesses.
Not being able to wash repeatedly	The germ will remain on me and lead to illness.	The scientific data show that washing once after potential exposure to germs, using warm (not hot!) water is all that is needed. Washing more can damage the protection of the skin. And if I refrain from putting my fingers in my eyes or mouth, I am not likely to allow the germs to enter my body.

minor bacterial infections. All of these are treatable and non-lethal in otherwise healthy individuals. Our immune systems, and sometimes medication, are capable of defeating the virus or infection.

Based on this, we were able to set up a fear ladder to help Chris begin to confront his fears. The situations were really a combination of touching certain things with increasing amounts of time to wait before washing. He rated his fear on the 5-point fear scale shown in chapter 4, where a rating of "5" is the most fear and "1" is no fear.

Chris's Fear Ladder

Situations	Fear level 1-5	Points earned
Not washing hands until touching any door handles, community property or others' belongings.	2	2
Touching door handles, community property, others' belongings, or something that fell to the floor and not washing for 5 minutes	3	3
Washing just once with warm water for about 20 seconds and rinsing for 10 seconds and then not washing again until the next time touching community property	3	3
Touching a door handle, community property, others' belongings, or something that fell to the floor and not washing for 10 minutes	4	4
Touching a door handle, community property, others' belongings, or something that fell to the floor and not washing for 20 minutes	4	4
Not washing before eating	5	5
Not washing for at least 20 minutes after using public restroom	5	5
Not washing hand for one full day	5	25
Points needed for video game purchase: 25		

The last three items on the fear ladder were not situations we wanted Chris to do regularly. Good hygiene dictates we wash before eating and after toilet use. However, the reason we included them was to demonstrate that even if he did not practice good hygiene, he would not get sick.

Chris earned points towards the purchase of new video games for facing each situation on his ladder. By facing several situations per day, he could earn a new game within a week's time. If he refrained from washing his hands for a whole day he immediately earned enough points for a new game.

Within about three weeks, Chris moved through all the situations except for the last one. At that point, we started an exercise program incorporating long walks with a parent and cycling. Although he would work up a mild sweat with these activities, the improved mood from exercising allowed him to finally go a whole day without washing. As expected, Chris did not get sick, allowing us to reinforce the notion that he was much safer from germs than he realized.

As I continued to work with Chris throughout the years, there were occasional flare ups of repetitive washing. These were usually triggered by greater school demands. For example, upon entering middle school, he showed more frustration with school work. He increased hand washing and had some social concerns about fitting in with new kids. By modifying work demands and creating a lunch-bunch group with matched peers, his stress level went down again along with his frequency of hand washing.

13 Somatic Symptom Disorder, and/or Illness Anxiety Disorder

Somatic symptom disorder and illness anxiety disorder may include real physical symptoms, but the worry, time, and energy devoted to caring for this symptom or preventing illness are excessive. Often, the way in which the symptom is managed creates more problems.

Darren was a 12-year-old with an average of one debilitating migraine headache per month, along with some milder headaches each week. Debilitating headaches required him to sit in a dark and quiet room, unable to do any activity, for anywhere from 1-to-3 hours. He was taking medication to prevent recurrent headaches.

About ten percent of school children have migraine headaches. Sixty percent of adolescents who suffer from migraines will continue to report periodic migraines after the age of thirty (according to the Migraine Research Foundation). Many children, such as Darren, develop anticipatory anxiety about having migraine attacks, causing them to avoid situations that were previously associated with headaches.

Darren would get an "aura" just prior to a headache, which included some dizziness, seeing colors, or blurred vision. Often, he would get this aura but then not get a headache. However, he started to avoid numerous situations in which he previously experienced the aura. These included socializing with friends at lunch, going to certain classes in school, and attending some after-school activities with friends.

In anticipation of a possible migraine, Darren would visit the school nurse many times per day, missing class time. At least once a week, he would ask to go home. Darren was also part of a lunch-time social skills group to work on connecting with peers. Although he was very good at conversing with the other kids and had made friends with them, he often did not attend the group or would ask to leave the group in order to see the nurse.

Interestingly, we noted that if we played a favored game in group, he would stay, but if the peers wanted to play a different game, he would report feeling strange and request a visit to the nurse. When his peers did not play his favorite game, Darren said that he felt strange and needed to see the nurse. This may not have been just an excuse. The situation may have caused stress, which is a known trigger for migraines.

We wanted to respect Darren's desire to avoid a painful migraine yet encourage him to still lead an active academic and social life. He had come to believe it was socializing and certain academic classes that led to migraines. Learning the true triggers to his migraines would be critical information.

For many children, lack of sleep, skipping meals, changes in weather, and stressful situations are triggers for migraines. For Darren, a goal of treatment was learning alternative ways to manage his stress level, without entirely avoiding academic and social situations.

To begin treatment, we acknowledged the painfulness and reality of his migraines. We also pointed out that he had associated these migraines with certain academic classes and socializing with peers because the aura had occurred in those situations. We suggested that it might not be the situations themselves that triggered the migraines, but how he managed them. Other factors (like lack of sleep or food) might also be the true culprits.

In discussing his perceptions of his academic classes, Darren explained that he often did not know how to do the work and feared the teacher would be mad at him, causing a migraine. In social situations, he had similar fears that peers might be mad at him, causing a migraine, if he did not know much about the topics they were discussing or did not know how to play the games they wanted to play. We helped him see some other ways to cope with these situations in order to reduce his stress. These are summarized in the "Think Like a Scientist" worksheet below.

Rather than avoiding classes, not socializing with peers, and escaping to the nurse, Darren learned that he could ask for help or just watch, not feel that he had to know everything. Knowing that he did not have to be perfect with peers and teachers allowed him to reduce his stress. Reducing stress made it less likely he would have a migraine.

Darren's Think Like a Scientist Summary

Feared situation	Anxious thought	Realistic outcome
Academic classes	If I don't understand, the teacher will be mad and I will get a migraine.	Teachers do not expect students to know everything and welcome questions. My teacher has told me it's okay to ask for assistance. I am not likely to get a migraine if I do not worry about the work so much.
Socializing with peers	Peers will be mad if I don't know what they are talking about or don't know how to play their games.	My friends will not mind if I am quiet or ask what they are talking about. If I do not know how to play a game, I can ask to just watch until I learn it, or play a different game. I am not likely to get a migraine if I do not feel like I have to be perfect with my friends.

We also started a mindfulness meditation program with Darren to help him reduce his stress level when needed. He explored a variety of meditation apps and practiced at bedtime every night. His parents also made sure that he got to bed early enough to get a good night's sleep, since lack of sleep is typically a trigger to migraines.

With these new coping tools, we created a fear ladder for Darren to take back his school and social life without being imprisoned by fear of migraines. This fear ladder included ways to cope with each situation.

Darren successfully worked through the fear ladder in about three weeks. He had some minor headaches in school and one major migraine at home after not sleeping well one night. He realized this migraine was more about sleep deprivation than any school or peer stress.

Darren's Fear Ladder

Situations	Fear level 1-5	Coping Tool
Attending class for a full period without leaving to go see the nurse.	2	Ask for help with work; ask if I can just watch; or meditate briefly if needed, rather than leave
Sit at lunch with peers	3	Sit quietly and just listen or watch rather than feeling like I have to participate
Go to afterschool or weekend activity with peers	4	Sit quietly and just listen or watch rather than feeling like I have to participate in all activities
Attend all classes without going to nurse	5	Ask for help with work, ask if I can just watch, or meditate briefly if needed rather than leave

Though migraines were still a part of his life, he had learned to function in school by managing his stress level through asking for help, not thinking he had to be perfect with peers, and by meditating. Instead of entirely avoiding class or peers, he was able to tolerate these situations with less stress.

14 Generalized Anxiety Disorder

A Case of Perfectionism and College Admissions Anxiety

Generalized Anxiety Disorder (GAD) refers to persistent worries (for at least six months) about a number of events or activities. Although GAD is not necessarily related to perfectionism, it is common that children with GAD tend to be perfectionistic and their worries to center around schoolwork performance. This chapter discusses the common challenges of perfectionistic thinking and its related anxiety.

 Don was a 16-year-old sophomore in high school with chronic worry about school work performance, grades, and the implications they might have for getting into college. He became extremely stressed about homework demands and his ability to comprehend classwork in school.

Don was often embarrassed to let teachers know that he did not fully understand the work. In addition, he worried about other kids teasing him, which had happened in the past. These two realms of worry on several occasions had led him to voice suicidal statements in school, which prompted his entering into treatment with me.

In our first visit, Don explained that, on several occasions, he had felt so bad that he had said he wished he were dead, but really had no intent of harming himself. He agreed to let his parents or me know if he felt that bad again. He explained that his sad feelings came as a result of falling behind in school.

He worried that he would never catch up and would get poor grades. That would prove that he was "stupid," and then he would not get into college or get a job. He also felt he was not likable because he had been recently teased by a boy who called him weird and stupid.

Together, we evaluated whether Don's fears about himself were true or false alarms, representing actual dangers or overestimations of negative events. We used the "Think Like a Scientist" strategy to evaluate his worries. Don was able to see that he did, indeed, have many friends, and that someone teasing him did not make him unlikable or stupid but, rather, made the teaser unlikable. Helping him with his work concerns, perfectionistic standards, insecurities about his intelligence, and anxiety about college was a bit more challenging.

For kids with perfectionistic attitudes towards their work and insecurities about their intelligence, I always like to introduce them to Carol Dweck's (2007) excellent work on children's theories of abilities such as intelligence and its effects on handling mistakes, motivation, and learning outcomes. Dweck distinguishes between two contrasting theories that individuals have about their abilities: a fixed mindset or a growth mindset.

A fixed mindset refers to the belief that qualities, like intelligence, are fixed traits. You are born with a certain amount of that quality, and it does not change much. Events like taking a test or getting a grade become either a confirmation or refutation of one's intelligence. Since making a mistake may indicate one is not smart enough, people with a fixed mindset prefer to do work they know they can do. They do not want to make a mistake or get help, which might imply that they are not intelligent.

A growth mindset refers to the belief that abilities, like intelligence, can be developed through effort and hard work—talent is only a starting point. Those with a growth mindset enjoy trying work that is a challenge. They welcome mistakes and assistance to learn more. Not suprisingly, Dweck (2007) shows that people with a growth mindset have better learning outcomes as they continue to seek out challenges, stay motivated in the face of mistakes, and accept help to learn more.

Here is a summary of Dweck's two mindsets and their-effects on learning.

The Effect of Mindset on Learning

Mindset	Preferred task difficulty	Response to mistakes	Acceptance of help	Learning outcomes
Fixed	Easy	Lose motivation	Avoid	Lower
Growth	Hard	Stay motivated	Welcome	Higher

The point of this important work is to show the perfectionist that trying difficult work, making mistakes, and then getting help to learn, is associated with better learning outcomes. In contrast, trying to be perfect, never making a mistake, and believing that mistakes or failure mean you are not smart, is not only wrong, but also leads to poorer outcomes.

Don and I discussed that falling behind in work or getting a poor grade was not a reflection of his intelligence. It was simply a sign to reach out for assistance. We spoke with the school to get extensions on work as needed, and for one class, we arranged to have a meeting with his teacher to go over content that Don did not fully understand. These were activities that would insure his growth as a learner and lead to better outcomes. In addition, we began to challenge his rigid beliefs about what it takes to get into college and eventually get a job.

It seems getting into a top college is not the only path to success. Frank Bruni (2015) in his book, *Where You Go Is Not Who You'll Be: An Antidote to the College*

Admissions Mania, shows that there are many paths to successful outcomes that do not necessarily involve getting into the most prestigious college. In fact, some studies show that getting into a top college has some positive effect on getting your first job but has very little effect on any subsequent jobs.

Not only may it be less important to get into the top colleges, it may, nevertheless, be easier to get into those top colleges than we have been led to believe. Statistics showing that top colleges are accepting lower percentages of college applications are quite misleading, according to a recent *New York Times* article (Carey, 2014). The truth is that high school students are applying to many more colleges than previously, resulting in colleges rejecting many more applications. While it is true that top colleges have lower application acceptance rates, the rate for qualified students getting into at least one of the top-rated colleges is a healthy 80%. The rate is even higher if you included all colleges, not just those that are top-rated.

The message here is this: About 80% of qualified students will get into a top college. If you are not qualified for a top college, there is still a college for you. The college to which you go does not determine your later success. Effort and motivation are larger determinants of later career success. These facts are sobering given the high level of anxiety imposed upon so many high school students in an effort to get into a great college.

Embracing these important points, we created a "Think Like a Scientist Summary" to help combat some of Don's worse fears.

Don continued to feel anxious when work piled up at school, or when he received a less-than-hoped-for grade. Each time, however, we worked through the Think Like a Scientist Summary until he was able to manage his anxiety, get needed assistance from school, and get back on track.

Don's Think Like a Scientist Summary

Feared situation	Anxious thought	Realistic outcome
Falling behind or getting a bad grade	If I fall behind, I will get bad grades, not get into college and not have a good career.	I can get an extension on work, and I can get help if I do not understand something. Poor grades one semester will not restrict my college choices. Poor grades my whole high school career may limit some college choices, but there is still a college I will be able to get into. And my college choice will not determine my later identity and career. My willingness to stay motivated and work hard (maintain a growth mindset) will determine my success later in life.
Someone teases me	It means I am unlikable and maybe unsafe	It is the teaser who is not likable. I have many friends. If the teaser continues, I can report it and I will not get in trouble but the teaser may, as it is against the laws of Harassment, Intimidation and Bullying. Teasers would be unwise to retaliate as they would get in much more trouble.

To help lower Don's overall level of anxiety, we got him on a regular exercise program. He joined the cross country track team in school. The team was not only great aerobic exercise, but also an excellent social outlet for him. There was a noticeable improvement in his anxiety on practice days.

We also introduced Don to a mindfulness meditation program, which not only helped to relax him when anxious, it also helped change his attitude about class and homework. Typically, Don would become distracted by worry while doing class and homework, thinking about whether he could complete it, understand it, fall behind, or forget to do some other work.

The mindfulness program helped him to engage more fully with whatever work he was doing, and he noticed that he actually got more done this way. By removing some of the worry that came with the work, he could actually enjoy and complete more work in a shorter period of time.

After about a year, it was clear that Don continued to feel anxious from time-to-time about school and peer relations, yet he now had effective tools to manage these feelings. Therefore, they did not escalate into crises and often subsided to a manageable level within a day.

15 Other Common Fears

So far, I have discussed fears related to many of the common anxiety disorders described in the *Diagnostic and Statistical Manual of Mental Disorders, 5th Edition* (DSM-5). However, there are many fears that do not fit neatly into a specific disorder. Nonetheless, these can be treated in much the same way, using fear ladders, rewards, "Think Like a Scientist" strategies, and relaxation tools.

Fear of others' aggression

One fear I have seen in many of my clients is a reaction to another's verbally or physically aggressive behavior. For example, Ned was a quiet, well-behaved 19-year-old in a special education high school for students with autism and related challenges. He was quite verbal, yet somewhat concrete in his thinking style.

He was often in class with students who had greater behavioral challenges than he, including those who argued with teachers and peers, shouted obscenities, and on occasion threw books, or knocked chairs over in anger. Understandably, Ned became quite anxious when any of these students "acted out."

There was some previous school history that likely contributed to his fears. Before attending his current high school, he was in a highly structured school program for verbally challenged, autistic children. In that environment, his classmates would suffer aversive punishments (such as blow horns sounded near their ears or Tabasco® sauce placed in their mouths) if they uttered inappropriate language. The school boasted an excellent record for "controlling" behaviors, yet few people knew of the punitive strategies it used. Most students could not tell their parents about the aversive and antiquated practices they witnessed. Ned was one of the few kids who had developed enough language that he could come home and tell his mother what was happening. We were able to get him out of that school and report those terrible practices to the board.

However, in the new school Ned continued to have an anxiety response anytime he saw students misbehave, either in school or out. He would utter "Uh oh" and ask to leave the situation right away. For example, if Ned's mom took him to the mall, and he saw a child misbehave, he would ask to leave the mall immediately. When interviewed about his experiences, he explained that he expected misbehaving students to be punished and that scared him.

We worked to help Ned see that the new school was different, and that kids would not be punished with blow horns or Tabasco sauce. If another student was too loud, Ned could leave briefly until the student calmed down. He still seemed concerned about the other student and worried that something bad would happen. Ned wanted to avoid going to class, riding the bus, or going to community-based instruction with some of the students who occasionally became upset.

Because Ned was a good reader, we developed a simplified "Think Like a Scientist" summary to help him cope with other students' outbursts.

Ned's Think Like a Scientist Summary for Others' Outbursts

Feared situation	Anxious thought	Realistic outcome
Student gets angry, curses, or shouts	The student or others will get hurt.	Sometimes people get angry. It usually only lasts about 1-5 minutes and then the student is calm again. If I stay away from the angry student, I will not get hurt. The student will not get hurt either. Teachers will show the student another way to handle the situation.

Ned learned that an outburst was temporary and that despite the noise, typically, no one was hurt. As a precaution, he learned to "stay away from an open flame," meaning give someone who is angry some space until he calms down. To help Ned stop avoiding situations where students sometimes had outbursts, we created a fear ladder. There were two students, Matt and Janet, who Ned most feared, since they were more likely to become upset. Ned did not request or need external rewards for confronting the rungs of the ladder. He wanted to be able to better cope with his anxiety about other students.

Ned's Fear Ladder for Others' Outbursts

Situations	Fear level 1-5	Coping Tool
Going to class or other programs with Matt or Janet.	2	People may get upset, but it is brief and no one gets hurt. I can leave if I need to.
Staying in the room for at least 1 minute when others are upset	4	People may get upset but it is usually done in a minute and no one gets hurt. I can keep a safe distance.
Staying in the room when others are upset for at least 5 minutes	5	People may get upset but it is almost always over in 5 minutes and no one gets hurt. I can keep a safe distance.

Ned successfully confronted each step on the ladder. When an outburst occurred, teachers reminded him that it would be brief, to try to tolerate it for 1-5 minutes, and to keep a safe distance. When the outburst was over, teachers reviewed with him how long it lasted and reminded Ned that no one had gotten hurt. This was to reinforce the coping tools he had developed.

Fear of unexpected changes in schedule or routine

Our 19-year-old high school student, Ned, also became upset when schedules or routines changed. If his parents told him they were taking a trip to see his grandmother at a certain time, he would frequently ask for reassurance about when they were leaving. Even after they told him multiple times and wrote it into a visual schedule, Ned would still ask repeatedly.

In addition to keeping to the scheduled time, Ned also demanded that planned routines not change. If traffic forced a change of route on the way to Grandma's house, he would become upset and insist on the route they originally planned, even if traffic made that next to impossible.

Ned needed events to run as scheduled and asked for constant reassurance about the time of those events. If a routine changed, he resisted, became upset, and insisted they stick to the originally planned routine.

One small way to help Ned deal with changes in schedule was to create a new visual schedule that showed any anticipated changes. This was only partially helpful, because Ned would now obsess over the new schedule, asking for reassurance of the timing of scheduled events.

We addressed his constant need for reassurance and fear of schedule changes in two ways. We used the "Think Like a Scientist" strategy to help Ned see that change would not be as bad as he thought, and we created a fear ladder to help him tolerate longer and longer periods of time without asking for reassurance.

Ned's Think Like a Scientist Summary for Changes

Feared situation	Anxious thought	Realistic outcome
Change in schedule or routine	I will not get to do what I want. Bad things may happen.	Although routines and schedules may change, most things remain the same. I will still be able to do most of what I want and I still have control over many things. For example, if our driving route changes, we will still get to our destination and I can still control the radio, windows, snacks, and temperature in the car.

Although Ned still seemed anxious when changes occurred, he actively began to cope by telling himself, "I can still control most of what happens." For the most part he stopped asking for constant reassurance, except on days when multiple changes occurred. Then he asked for some reassurance because he feared other things might also change.

Ned was also an avid cycler and meditator. Both the physical activity and the meditations had a noticeable positive effect on lowering his anxiety about change and dealing with others' outbursts.

Ned's Fear Ladder for Tolerating Time Without Reassurance

Situations	Fear level 1-5	Coping Tool
Not asking parents or staff about schedule for 10 minutes after seeing the schedule.	2	I know schedule already and if it changes, I can still get most of what I want.
Not asking parents or staff about schedule for 20 minutes after seeing the schedule.	3	I know schedule already and if it changes, I can still get most of what I want.
Not asking parents or staff about schedule for 60 minutes after seeing the schedule.	4	I know schedule already and if it changes, I can still get most of what I want.
Not asking parents or staff about schedule at all after seeing the schedule for the day.	5	I know schedule already and if it changes, I can still get most of what I want.

16 Summary of Key Points

I started this book by describing the science of over-coming anxiety. The common ingredient in successful anxiety treatments is "gradual exposure," that is, gradually facing feared situations until the fear subsides. In clinical practice, it is not always clear how you get an individual to face his most dreaded fears. This is where the art of therapy comes in, learning what to do and say to win over clients to cooperate in facing their fears.

Treatment starts with motivation

In chapter 3, I describe ways to prepare verbal clients to engage in treatment by first increasing awareness of their strengths to give hope of an optimistic future and to lessen the threat of examining challenges (such as anxiety) that may interfere with accomplishing their goals. In addition, educating clients about their alarm system (that signals danger) can help them begin to question whether the danger that they fear is truly a danger.

Explaining how the alarm system can lead to false alarms allows clients to understand how they can be so physically fearful, even though there may, in fact, be no real danger. Finally, helping clients to change their goal from getting rid of anxiety to not being controlled by anxiety helps set them up for success. We all will be anxious at times, but do not want to be held hostage to such emotions.

For less verbal clients, motivation is very much about providing incentives or rewards for facing fears. Using rewards is not just for less verbal individuals, but also for many children who may not comprehend the natural rewards of facing fears, such as having more freedom and accomplishing more goals in life. Kids may need a more immediate and concrete reward to begin facing fearful situations.

Identify specific fears and create a fear ladder

The next key to treatment involves identifying the exact situations the individual fears and creating a "ladder" from least to most fearful. For verbal individuals, we can have them rate how fearful they are of each situation to determine the order of steps on the ladder. For less verbal individuals, we can use their avoidance or protest behavior to rate how challenging each situation is.

For example, the diabetic child who was afraid to have his blood drawn only began to withdraw his arm from the lancet when it was 60 cm (about 2 feet) from his finger. Thus, 60 cm became the first step of the fear ladder.

Chapters 7-15 described fear ladders for many common anxiety disorders. Verbal individuals should rate their anxiety level before and after each exposure to a situation. This not only allows them to see that their anxiety diminishes, but the act of rating also provides an opportunity to observe the anxious response from a distance, perhaps allowing them to reflect on how to alter that response.

Develop tools to help cope with and face fears

A major tool to lowering anxiety enough to face fears is learning to "Think Like a Scientist." This cognitive behavioral strategy focuses on challenging two parts of most worries: overestimating how likely it is that the feared event will occur, and overestimating how bad it would really be if the feared event occurred.

Chapters 7-15 show many examples of how my clients developed "Think Like a Scientist" summaries to help them face their fears.

In addition to challenging one's worrisome thoughts, there are numerous ways to calm an anxious mind. Exercise and busy-work are active ways of calming and distracting from anxious thoughts. Deep breathing, progressive muscle relaxation, and mindfulness meditations are examples of quieter ways to calm the mind. In addition to the relaxation guides I have provided in chapter 5, there are many websites and apps to explore that offer free meditation and relaxation guides. I listed some in chapter 5, yet the interested reader can find more by searching online for "free meditation guides."

When challenging worrisome thoughts and relaxation strategies do not yield enough relief, consider the use of neurofeedback, medication, or both, to lower anxiety. Neurofeedback is quite safe in general, yet there is a cost and time commitment that may not make it everyone's first choice. The research on its effectiveness is promising, yet more outcome studies are needed to determine how effective it will be. Medications similarly may not be a first choice since they always carry the risk of side effects. However, medications are sometimes quite useful in lowering anxiety sufficiently to allow individuals to face previously feared situations.

Consider the big picture!

Sometimes we need to explore a child's environment to see what else may be making a child anxious that is not obvious from the reported symptoms. For example, students may have an increase in OCD symptoms or specific phobias when they are under greater stress from heavier school-work demands. I have seen many students experience a reduction in anxiety symptoms when the demands of school work were modified to align with the child's current capabilities. This simple example points to another key issue: sometimes the environment, not the child, needs to change. If a child is in a dangerous situation, being bullied, abused, or neglected, these are real dangers. Treatment must focus on creating safe environments for the child. As a consequence of trauma, a child may persist in fearing situations that are now safe. Helping children distinguish between the dangers of the past and safety in the present is part of healing.

The ultimate goal

All of the information in this book is meant to help children and teens have greater control over the choices they make each day. Though they may not be able to rid themselves of anxiety, they can learn not to be controlled by it. By challenging worrisome thoughts with science, becoming more mindful of thoughts and bodily sensations, learning tools to calm, and gradually facing fears, our children and teens can be free to pursue their interests and dreams.

References

Baker, J. E. (2008). *No More Meltdowns*. Arlington, TX: Future Horizons, Inc.

Baker, J. E. (2001). *Social Skills Picture Book*. Arlington, TX: Future Horizons, Inc.

Barlow, D. (2004). *Anxiety and Its Disorders: the Nature and Treatment of Anxiety and Panic*. 2d ed. New York: Guilford Press.

Blumenthal, J. A., M. A. Babyak, K. A. Moore, W.E. Craighead, S. Herman, P. Khatri, R. Waugh, M. A. Napolitano, L. M. Forman, M. Appelbaum, P. M. Doraiswamy, and K. R. Krishnan (1999). Effects of exercise training on older patients with major depression. Arch Intern Med. Oct 25;159(19):2349-56.

Bruni, F. (2015). *Where You Go Is Not Who You'll Be: An Antidote to the College Admissions Mania*. New York: Grand Central Publishing.

Burns, D. D. (1981). *Feeling good: The new mood therapy*. New York: New American Library.

Carey, K. (2014). For accomplished students, reaching a good college isn't as hard as it seems. *New York Times*. New York edition. Nov 30, SR2.

Dweck, C. (2007). *Mindset: The New Psychology of Success*. New York: Random House.

Ferber, R. (2006). *Solve Your Child's Sleep Problems.* New York: Simon and Schuster.

Ferber, R. (1985). *Solve Your Child's Sleep Problems.* New York: Simon and Schuster.

Goleman, Daniel (1995). *Emotional Intelligence.* New York: Bantam Books.

Hammond, D. C. (2005). Neurofeedback treatment of depression and anxiety. Journal of Adult Development, Vol. 12, Nos. 2/3, DOI: 10.1007/s10804-005-7029-5.

Huebner, D. and B. Matthews. (2007). *What to Do When Your Brain Gets Stuck: A Kid's Guide to Overcoming OCD.* Washington, DC: Magination Press.

Jacobson, E. (1938). *Progressive Relaxation.* Chicago: University of Chicago Press.

Kagan, Jerome. (1997). Galen's Prophecy: Temperament in Human Natures. Boulder, CO: Westview Press.

Kranowitz, C. (2006). *The Out-of-Sync Child Has Fun: Activities for Kids with Sensory Processing Disorder.* New York: Perigee.

Meiklejohn, J., C. Phillips, M. L. Freedman, M. L. Griffin, G. Biegel, A. Roach, J. Frank, C. Burke, L. Pinger, G. Soloway, R. Isberg, R., E. Sibinga, L. Grossman, and A Saltzman, A. (2012). Integrating mindfulness training into K-12 education: fostering the resilience of teachers and students. Mindfulneşs, Volume 3, Issue 4, pp 291-307.

Migraine Research Foundation. (n.d.). Retrieved April 13, 2015, from http://www.migraineresearchfoundation.org/Migraine in Children.html

Otto, M., and J. A. J. Smits. (2011). *Exercise for Mood and Anxiety: Proven Strategies for Overcoming Depression and Enhancing Well-Being.* Oxford University Press.

Rapee, R., A. Wignall, S. Spence, H. Lyneham, V. Cobham. (2008). *Helping Your Anxious Child: A Step-by-Step Guide for Parents.* 2d ed. Oakland, CA: New Harbinger Publications.

Shabani, D.B and W. W. Fisher. (2006). Stimulus fading and differential reinforcement for the treatment of needle phobia in youth with autism. J of Applied Behavior Analysis, 39(4), 449-452.

Thomas, A. and S. Chess. (1977). *Temperament and Development.* New York: Brunner/Mazel.

Uhlenhuth E.H., V. Starcevic, T. D. Warner, W. Matuzas, T. McCarty, B. Roberts, S. Jenkusky. (2002). A general anxiety-prone cognitive style in anxiety disorders. J Affect Disord. Aug;70(3):241-9.

Illustrations

Alarm	© valentint / Fotolia
Joe	© Lisa F. Young / Fotolia
Boy on Ladder	© Pete Pahham / Fotolia
Anxiety Word Cloud	© intheskies / Fotolia
Fear Scale	Jed Baker
Find Letters	Jed Baker
iPad	Michael Coté
Ellie	© altanaka / Fotolia
Kyle	© Sabphoto / Fotolia
Katie	© lu-photo / Fotolia
Jonathan	© yuu / Fotolia
Mandy	© Rommel Canlas / Innovated Captures / Fotolia
Arlene	© Galina Barskaya / Fotolia
Chris	© Caroline Schiff / Blend Image / Fotolias
Darren	© Sabphoto / Fotolia
Don	© Lisa F. Young / Fotolia
Ned	© Laurent Hamels / Fotolia